Fraud Prevention Techniques for
CREDIT CARD FRAUD

The Professional's Guide to
Preventing Credit Card Fraud in E-Commerce,
Mail Order and Telephone Order Sales

By David Montague

CREDIT CARD FRAUD

The Professional's Guide to
Preventing Credit Card Fraud in E-Commerce,
Mail Order and Telephone Order Sales

CREDIT CARD FRAUD

The Professional's Guide to
Preventing Credit Card Fraud in E-commerce,
Mail Order and Telephone Order Sales

David Montague

Trafford Publishing
Victoria, BC, Canada

This book is available at quantity discounts for bulk purchases.
For information, call 1-866-752-6820 available 9-5 pst

Further information about Preventing Credit Card Fraud and David Montague can be found at www.fraudpractice.com

Note for Librarians: a cataloguing record for this book that includes Dewey Classification and US Library of Congress numbers is available from the National Library of Canada. The complete cataloguing record can be obtained from the National Library's online database at: www.nlc-bnc.ca/amicus/index-e.html

ISBN 1-4120-1460-3

TRAFFORD

This book was published on-demand in cooperation with Trafford Publishing.
On-demand publishing is a unique process and service of making a book available for retail sale to the public taking advantage of on-demand manufacturing and Internet marketing. On-demand publishing includes promotions, retail sales, manufacturing, order fulfilment, accounting and collecting royalties on behalf of the author.

Suite 6E, 2333 Government St., Victoria, B.C. V8T 4P4, CANADA

Phone 250-383-6864	Toll-free 1-888-232-4444 (Canada & US)
Fax 250-383-6804	E-mail sales@trafford.com
Web site www.trafford.com	TRAFFORD PUBLISHING IS A DIVISION OF TRAFFORD HOLDINGS LTD.
Trafford Catalogue #03-1838	www.trafford.com/robots/03-1838.html

10   9   8   7   6   5   4   3   2

Contents

Part III
Fraud-Prevention Techniques:
32 of the most used fraud-prevention techniques

Acknowledgements

This book is the culmination of over 11 years of learning, consulting and teaching. During that time my peers, customers, friends and prospects have helped me develop into who I am. I owe thanks to all of them for their support, and could not have written this book without them.

I want to express my thanks to Joe Richards, who gave me my first real opportunity in consulting, and who had the foresight to see my talent and ability when my business background was still very junior. Joe recently passed away, but his memory, kindness and spirit live on.

I would also like to thank Mike Brecheisen for his unwavering support and friendship. Mike and I have worked together for years and he has been instrumental in my career development. More importantly, the friendship we have formed along the way has taught me how to have fun at work.

Likewise, I have to thank Bill Mckeirnan, the CEO of CyberSource Corporation, for the freedom and confidence he showed in me to pursue and develop solutions for preventing credit card fraud. Bill has always given me the latitude I needed to set new goals and pursue better solutions. His confidence and drive have been invaluable.

Finally I have to thank my family — most importantly my wife Carrie — for her support and patience as I spent so much or our "quality" time writing this book. Carrie has been a personal, as well as a professional, inspiration to me in writing this book.

Credit Card Fraud

Introduction

Fraud is nothing new to the merchant. Since the beginning of time, man has always looked for the opportunity to defraud others — to gain goods or services without making payment. For the credit card industry, fraud is a part of doing business, and is something that is always a challenge. The merchants that are the best at preventing fraud are the ones that can adapt to change quickly.

This book is written to provide information about how to prevent credit card fraud in the card-not-present space (mail order, telephone order, e-commerce). This book is meant to be an introduction to combating fraud, providing the basic concepts around credit card payment, the ways fraud is perpetrated, along with write ups that define and provide best practices on the use of 32 fraud-prevention techniques.

Card-Present vs. Card-Not-Present

Credit card purchases are described as either being "card-present" or "card-not-present." The difference between the two is the presence of the physical card. If a merchant processes a transaction in which the consumer physically gives them the card to process the order, the transaction is considered card-present. If the merchant doesn't take physical possession of the card to process the order, such as in the case of a telephone order, it is considered a card-not-present transaction.

So who pays when a fraudster steals goods and services? It may surprise you to find out the merchant is left with the bill in most of the cases. For purchases at a physical store in which the consumer comes in and buys goods and services with a credit card, we call this purchase a card-present transaction. In this transaction a consumer hands a merchant the physical card.

When the goods and services are sold to a consumer and the physical card is not given to the merchant, for instance they phone in an order ("Telephone Order") or make a purchase through a catalogue ("Mail Order"), they are conducting what is called a card-not-present transaction. Mail order and telephone orders are typically lumped together in a category we call MOTO. The sale of goods and services online, called "e-commerce," is also a member of this group.

This book focuses on the prevention of fraud for the card-not-present transaction. The payment process, fraud schemes, and fraud techniques will all focus on these types of transactions. In some cases comparative views of card-present to card-not-present is made, but for the most part I only talk to the card-not-present transaction. It is important to understand the fraud-prevention techniques used in the card-present world do not translate to the card-not-present world. There are a number of books and references available for preventing fraud in the card-present space, but very few resources for the card-not-present space. The specific fraud-prevention techniques discussed in this book are designed specifically for the card-not-present space, and will provide far better results for merchants.

In terms of orders processed, far more orders are processed in the card-present space than the card-not-present space. While the card-not-present space represents less than 1/3 of the total credit card purchases annually, the e-commerce space is showing significant year-over-year growth. Today e-commerce orders represent a very small percentage of the total card-not-present transactions occurring annually, but as you explore and expand into this channel it is important that you have the processes and tools to prevent fraud losses.

In terms of fraud, the incidence of fraud in the card-not-present channel is far greater than the card-present channel. Orders given in the card-not-present channel are far riskier for a merchant because the fraudster is anonymous to you.

Your Background with Fraud

If you are new to the fraud space, you are probably feeling a little overwhelmed. But don't despair — with the right tools you can quickly make a difference for your company. Everyone assumes the other guy has a great fraud-prevention process in place, but in reality everyone could use some help.

This book was written with the concept of a "Fraud Practitioner" in mind. A fraud practitioner is a person who is actively engaged in defining, managing and monitoring fraud-prevention practices for a business. These individuals may or may not have a background in preventing fraud, security or criminology, but they do have responsibility for stopping fraud.

From my experience working with merchants all over the world, I have seen many different departments in an organization that are responsible for the set up and management of fraud prevention for the business. Likewise, the individuals tasked with setting up and supporting a fraud-prevention strategy come from a variety of backgrounds, including customer service, finance and accounting, information technology. Only some come from actual fraud, criminal or security backgrounds.

It is important to understand that you will need input and assistance from multiple departments to build an effective fraud-prevention strategy. Customer Service, Sales, Information Technology, Finance, Operations and Legal Departments all have a role to play. You have to integrate these departments into your plans to ensure that the impact of your new business processes and fraud-prevention techniques are well understood and can be interwoven with their goals.

Regardless of the department you report to, and your background with fraud, I have taken a lot of effort in this book to keep the concepts and explanations easy to understand. I have also provided many examples to illustrate fraud schemes and to help visualize how fraud techniques are used.

How to Use this Book

If you are new to fraud, start from the beginning of this book and work your way through it, and you will find that each chapter will build on what you learned before. When you are done you will have a good foundation on preventing fraud. For the more advanced fraud practitioner, you may use this book more as a reference tool, to look up certain techniques or schemes.

Before you can successfully build an effective strategy to combat fraud, you have to understand the business processes and techniques that are available to you. This book is the first in a series, and is intended to provide you with the foundation you will need to build an effective strategy. In this book I focus on the payment process, the anatomy of fraud and the most common fraud techniques in the industry. Beyond understanding what the techniques are, I discuss how you can use them, and provide some best-practice advice so you can implement them.

Once you read this book you will find yourself coming back to it as a reference to brush up on fraud-prevention techniques and how to use them.

Part I

Credit Card (Card-Not-Present) Payment
How merchants get paid for goods and services

How do you begin to understand card-not-present fraud, and the mechanics behind it? You start with the card-not-present payment process. This gives you a good basic understanding of the touch points in an order and the people and organizations that facilitate those touch points. Through this you see how the fraudster can manipulate these people and business processes to their advantage.

Don't short-change yourself on understanding this process. Too often I see that fraudsters understand the business processes around payment better than the merchant does — and you can't afford that. You don't have to be an expert in credit card payment, but you had better understand the basics, or you will struggle in developing an effective strategy. How will you know where the best points are to implement fraud-prevention techniques if you don't understand the payment process? How will you know how to balance your fraud-prevention goals with the sales and administration goals if you don't understand the impact of your strategies on the payment process?

You will also find you need to understand the payment process because you and your staff will naturally gravitate to what they know best. I point this out because if you are like most merchants out there, you probably don't come from a law enforcement background. Depending on your background and the background of your team, you will find certain topics in developing your new fraud-prevention strategy more difficult than others.

Think about the background of you and others on your team. If they came from the website development or content teams, they will understand the buy page and shopping cart. If they came from the credit or finance side, they will understand the money flow, but not how the order gets placed or filled. If they came from the call center, they will understand the order page, but not where it goes from there. You, as the fraud practitioner, are responsible for making sure everyone on the team understands how fraud touches all of these points. You are also the one that has to create a seamless fraud-prevention business process that spans all these departments.

Remember, although your primary goal is fraud prevention and reduction, that is not every department's goal. Envision three major goals in a business: increase revenue, lower costs and reduce losses. These goals can be in direct conflict, and your job is really to balance these goals to ensure maximum "profitability" to the company.

A good way to understand this is to look at it from a sales, finance and operations perspective. Your Finance Department is going to be focused on profitability, and profitability means looking at how much the business is losing, how much they are spending to manage the processes today, and what the impact is on revenue. In working with your Finance Department, you have to be prepared to explain the impact of any changes in terms of profitability.

Your Operations and Customer Service Departments will be focused on managing administration costs. In working with them, you can expect to get questions about associated head counts. Does your new strategy reduce the need for people? Does it increase the head count? Does it add any costs to completing sales, such as transaction costs?

Your Sales Department will be focused on sales conversion, making sure they can get every possible sale they can. Those fraudulent orders still represent sales to them, so they are very leery of anything that might kill a potential sale. You will have to show the sales force that your efforts are not barriers to sales and are not "insulting" good customers.

For all of these departments, fraud is not their primary goal, so you have to be the champion to get them to feel the pain and to help in finding the right solution to stop fraud.

In Part 1 we discuss these organizations, departments and roles involved in the payment process. We also cover the steps the money goes through to get to your business and finally we start our discussion on charge-backs and your liability as a merchant.

Chapter 1

Understanding the Players: Associations, Banks, Payment Processors, Gateways, Merchants and Consumers

Each of the players in the payment process has a role to fulfill. They are performing these roles to make money. Understanding this will help you in working with them. In this chapter we will discuss each of the major players in terms of what their role is, which other players they associate or represent and how they make money.

There are seven major players in the payment process: consumers, merchants, issuing banks, acquiring banks, payment processors, gateway services and card associations.

Consumers & Merchants

Let's start with two everyone is familiar with, the "consumer" and "merchant." The consumer is an individual or organization that has the intent of making a purchase. They have money or credit and they desire goods and services. The merchant is the one with the goods and services and is looking to sell them to consumers.

Now the consumer can be motivated to select a particular merchant by several things: price, service, selection or preference. But the merchant's main motivation is to make money. The merchant is in business to make money and they do so by selling the goods or services for more money than they bought them. This money between what they bought it for and what they sold it for is called their margin.

There are a lot of different ways to exchange money for services, bartering, cash, checks, debit cards, installment payments or credit cards. Our focus is on credit cards and with credit cards, the consumer and the merchant both have banks that they are working with that manage the credit card payment transactions.

Issuing Bank

The consumer got his credit card from a bank or credit union, called the "issuing bank." Sometimes you may hear an issuing bank being called an "issuer," which means the same thing. The issuing bank is not just associated with major credit card brands such as American Express, MasterCard and Visa, but also with credit cards called "private label credit cards." These are the ones that department stores or shops offer, such as Sears and Target cards.

Issuing banks are lending institutions that work behind these credit cards to grant and manage the extended credit. Some examples of these are Bank of America, Citibank, MBNA, Household Financial, GE and Wells Fargo.

The purpose of the issuing bank is to grant credit directly to a consumer. They are the ones that have a consumer fill out an application, check a consumer's credit history and maintain their account. The issuing bank is the one that decides what a consumer's credit limit is, based on credit history and current debt load. There are literally thousands of issuing banks in the United States — any bank or credit union you see on the corner could be an issuer. In Canada and the United Kingdom there are far fewer banks, so the number of issuing banks is much smaller.

What motivates the issuing bank? They are in it for the money as well. They make money on the interest the consumer pays on outstanding balances from previous purchases, and they get a part of every purchase a consumer makes with the card from a merchant.

Acquiring Bank

The acquiring bank represents the merchant. They process all of the merchant's credit card payments with the associations (American Express, MasterCard, Visa..), and provide the merchant with reconciliation tools. The acquiring bank makes money on every transaction a merchant processes.

There are number of acquiring banks in the United States and abroad, and merchants are free to move from one acquirer to another. Merchants typically select their acquiring bank based on the amount of money, called basis points, they charge per transaction.

Payment Processors & Gateway Services

There is nothing stopping a merchant from directly connecting to their acquiring bank, but there are a number of reasons why they may not want, or be able, to. There are technical and business requirements in conducting the payment process for credit cards, and most merchants don't want to have to worry about these requirements. Instead they choose to use a third party between them and their acquiring banks. These third parties are called payment processors and gateway services.

Payment processors offer the physical infrastructure for the merchant to communicate with the acquiring banks and the associations. They are the ones that connect everyone together. This allows some very small banks to offer merchant services that they could not provide on their own. Payment processors make their money by charging a flat transaction fee or by charging basis points to the merchant. Some payment processors also provide acquiring bank services directly.

Gateway services offer merchants physical infrastructure as well. They typically offer technology and integration services that are faster, easier and less expensive to get started. They also give the merchant the freedom to move between acquiring banks so they can negotiate better rates without having to make changes to their production systems. The gateway service provider will charge a transaction fee or basis points for their services. These fees are on top of the payment processor fees the merchant is already paying.

If a merchant decides to use a gateway service provider they will still have to set up accounts with an acquirer. The acquirer could be an acquiring bank or a payment processor that offers acquiring.

Card Associations

Finally there are card associations, such as Visa, MasterCard International, American Express and Discover. There are a lot more — this is just a sampling. The card associations are responsible for setting up the guidelines on how transactions, services and disputes are to be handled. They interface with national banking laws and provide the money that covers some of the fraud that occurs within the membership. Each association runs a little differently, so one size does not fit all.

Visa has regions that operate pretty much autonomously. There is Visa U.S.A., Visa Europe, Visa Asia, etc. Each of these regions may have slightly different rules, tools and services they offer. Visa does not actually issue credit cards to consumers; they use issuing banks to issue credit cards that are branded as "Visa."

MasterCard International is a little different from Visa in that it is one association for the entire globe: all regions go into the same structure. This has some benefits when it comes to regulations and tools. MasterCard International also uses issuing banks to issue credit cards to consumers that are branded as "MasterCard."

American Express differs even more by acting as the issuer for all American Express branded credit cards. American Express is one global organization with regional coverage. American Express also differs from Visa and MasterCard in allowing merchants to set up direct connections for performing the acquiring functions.

One of the side notes that should be understood is the concept of "co-branding." Today consumers have credit cards that are being sponsored by airlines, car companies, local clubs, etc. These organizations get a little of the money for each purchase. In some cases it may be that the organization is actually the Issuer, but in a lot of cases it is an actual issuing bank that is offering a number of co-branded credit cards for consumers to choose from. The card is still an American Express, Visa or MasterCard.

Each of these credit card associations has their own network of systems, policies for use and payment processing. Each of these associations develops new fraud-prevention tools and tries to get merchants to adopt them. These fraud-prevention practices are only good for that type of card. Usually if good market adoption occurs, the other cards will adopt a similar technology.

The actual fraud programs and services an association offers changes often, and you should check out their websites often to learn more about the types of fraud-prevention services and solutions they are endorsing.

Conclusion

Aside from the consumers, all of the players we have discussed rely on consumers to make purchases; because they make their money each time the consumer makes a purchase. For each consumer purchase the merchant is trying to make profit from a percentage of money called their margin, which represents the difference between what it cost them to buy and sell the goods and what they sold it for to the consumer.

In that margin the merchant has to pay for all of their overhead, staff, utilities, property, loss, insurance etc.... Profit comes from the margin and the merchant needs that margin to go a long way before they actually make profit, so every penny of it counts.

There is no denying that a merchant makes less profit on an order paid by credit card than by cash. But all merchants understand that having the ability to take credit cards means there are a lot more potential sales that would have never been possible as strictly cash deals. The merchant's additional costs for credit card transactions come from interchange rates and basis points.

The issuing banks, acquiring banks, associations, and sometimes the payment processors, all get their money from the merchant in terms of basis points paid by the merchant. Basis points are percentage points of a sale a merchant pays on every purchase made with a credit card to the acquiring bank. Merchants negotiate with their acquiring banks, and sometimes the associations, to get the best possible interchange rates and basis points. The key point to understand is all of the players, aside from the consumer, have a vested interest in each consumer purchase.

Another key take-away from this chapter is to really understand that fraud is not defined or felt the same by all players in the payment process. Consumers worry about identity theft and having to rebuild their credit, while merchants worry about losing goods and having to pay fines. Acquiring banks worry about collusive merchants working with fraudsters to defraud the banks. Issuers worry about fraudulent applications, counterfeit cards and stolen cards. Associations worry about how fraud will impact their brand name to consumers, merchants and banks. So when talking, reading or evaluating fraud-prevention techniques remember to check whose perspective you are getting.

	Represents	Paid From
Consumer		
Merchant		Consumer
Issuing Bank	Consumer	Consumer, Merchant
Acquiring Bank	Merchant	Merchant
Payment Processor	Merchant, Acquiring Banks	Merchant
Gateway Service	Payment Processors, Acquiring Banks, Merchants	Merchant
Card Association	Issuers, Acquirers, Merchants	Issuers, Acquirers, Merchants

Chapter 2

The Money Flow

What does money flow and credit cards have to do with fraud prevention? In a cash society a merchant never cared about who the consumer was. With the introduction of credit cards the merchant took on new responsibilities for authenticating consumers, showing proof of sales and providing service and support after the sale. For most merchants having to authenticate the consumer before taking their cash, or having to worry about a bank coming back after the sale and taking the money bank, was a foreign concept. The concept of fraud went from just physically securing their shops to having to spot fraud in the money flow.

To understand the money flow you need an understanding of the business processes and steps an order goes through for money and goods to exchange hands. With cash the consumer hands a merchant cash, the merchant performs checks to make sure it is not counterfeit, and calculates the change. With that done the consumer is on their way. If a consumer returns the goods, the merchant simply has to pay the consumer back in cash. There are no third parties in the process — everything occurs between a merchant and consumer.

With credit cards we introduce new complexities into processing an order:

- **Do you accept the card?** With a cash transaction the merchant can immediately see if the currency the consumer is trying to use is a currency they accept. If you are in the United States and a consumer tries to make a purchase with Euros the merchant will tell them they don't accept Euros. With credit cards, there are also a lot of different credit card types, and as a merchant you need to know which ones you can process. Your acquiring bank will only support a certain group of these cards, and you need to make sure you can process the card prior to accepting them from the consumer.

- **Is the card real?** With cash, most people are very familiar with how it looks and feels. There are a number of things a merchant can do to see if the cash is counterfeit, but, in general, everyone knows what a one dollar bill is. For credit cards, there are different brands, different logos, colors, and names on them. To make it even more difficult, banks and associations change these looks often. Likewise the credit card only has a set of numbers across the front of it — how do you know these numbers aren't just gibberish?

- **Does the consumer have money available on the card?** When you take cash you know immediately if the consumer has enough money to pay for the purchase. With credit cards, there is no "value remaining" indicator on the card. With credit cards a merchant has to go out and ask if the consumer has money remaining.

- **Is this consumer authorized to use this particular credit card?** When a credit card is used, there is no magic check occurring on the names authorized to use the credit card. If the credit card says John Smith, how do you know this is really John Smith?

- **Have you delivered the goods or services?** If not, you cannot ask for your money. This is because with credit cards there are rules about when you can request to have funds paid to you, and how you have to handle customer service complaints. With cash you can have consumers pre-pay for special orders, split shipments and delay shipments, but you cannot do these things with credit cards.

Now instead of a transaction occurring between a merchant and consumer, there can be up to seven entities (merchants, consumers, issuing banks, acquiring banks, payment processors, gateway services, card associations) involved in a transaction. As a merchant you have to rely on third parties to make sure the consumer can pay for the transaction, and to authenticate that the consumer is authorized to make the purchase.

Having so many more entities involved in a transaction means there are more steps a merchant has to go through to collect their money on a transaction.

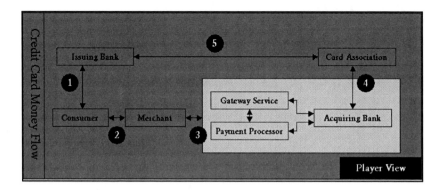

1. The consumer contacts an issuing bank and opens a credit card account. They are issued a credit card with a unique account number and a credit line (which is how much they are allowed to spend on the account).
2. A consumer goes to a merchant and selects goods or services to be purchased. He or she provides the credit card information to pay for the transaction.
3. The merchant takes the credit card information provided by the consumer and attempts to validate it through tests and checks and sends it to the acquiring bank to find out if the consumer has money available on the credit card to make the purchase. How the information is routed to the acquiring bank depends on the merchant's decision to use a gateway service or payment processor. Remember a gateway service and payment processor operate as a middleman in the transaction giving value-added services to the merchant. The merchant could be using any of the following methods to get their credit card orders out to the acquiring bank:
   a. Directly connect to the acquiring bank
   b. Connecting to a payment processor that connects out to an acquiring bank
   c. Connecting to a gateway service that connects out to an acquiring bank
   d. Connecting to a gateway service that connects out to a payment processor that connects to an acquiring bank
   e. Connecting to a payment processor that offers acquiring bank services directly
4. The acquiring bank routes a request through the card association physical network to the issuing bank to see if funds are available on the consumer's credit card.

5. The issuing bank checks the consumer's credit line and if funds are available they will set aside the amount of money that the order requires for payment. This money is "reserved" only – it has not changed hands, and is not the merchant's money yet. At this point a reply is sent back through the card association network to the acquiring bank, then back to the merchant to let them know the status of the request for funds.

All of this has gone on, and all we have done is determine that the card is a valid credit card and that the consumer has enough money available on their credit card to make the purchase. There are seven major steps associated with processing a card-not-present credit card purchase. The previous graphic and example depict only the first two steps in that process. The merchant still hasn't gotten paid for their goods or services. Additionally the merchant has to worry about the "reserve" on their funds expiring, credits and potential bad transactions, called "charge-backs."

The remainder of this chapter will discuss each of these seven steps in more detail, but let's take a brief look at the seven steps in processing a credit card transaction to get you familiar with the big picture.

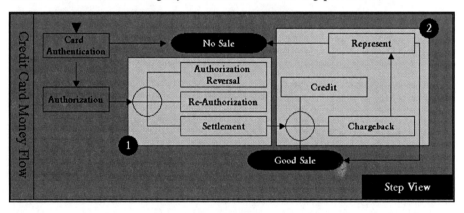

In the Step View graphic I highlight two major areas in grey that represent two conceptual phases in the credit card process: pre-payment (1) and post payment (2). The pre-payment phase shows all of the steps that can happen on a consumer's order before the merchant receives money from their credit card. The post-payment phase shows all of the steps that can happen on a consumer's order after the merchant has received money.

*   **Card Authentication** – Validate the credit card number the consumer gave you to verify that it's actually a real credit card

number and not just a bunch of random numbers. If the consumer fails this test, no sale. If the consumer passes this test, the order moves to authorization.

- **Authorization** - Check for and "reserve" funds on the consumer's credit card for the order.
- **Authorization Reversal** - Contacting the issuing bank to "un-reserve" funds on a consumer's credit card if they decide not to make the purchase.
- **Settlement** - Request for physical payment of funds from the consumer's credit card.
- **Credit** - The return of physical payment of funds back to the consumer's credit card.
- **Charge-back** - A request from the issuing bank to provide additional documentation on a consumer's order to prove the consumer made the purchase. These requests can be based on customer service issues or suspected fraud.
- **Represent** - The presentation of additional documentation to the issuing bank to prove the consumer made the actual purchase.

Remember not all seven steps will occur with every transaction. The Step View graphic provided a quick overview of the seven steps and the major objective of each step. Even with the data you will receive in the remainder of this chapter, make sure you work with your acquiring bank to get more detailed information on the policies and procedures they have in place for these steps.

Card Authentication

Before you can check to see if the consumer has money available, you need to make sure the card number they gave you is a valid credit card number, and you do this by doing a "card authentication." This is where you check to make sure the card number you were given by a consumer could even possibly be a credit card number and not just a random set of numbers. The card authentication check is not trying to see if the account is real, or what money is available on it — it is just making sure the numbers the consumer gave you fit the normal credit card pattern and range.

Card authentication is typically accomplished by using a test called a MOD 10 check. This check is built into many payment systems, and is typically found on the buy page of a website. This will catch things like too few, or too many, digits or an incorrect arrangement of the digits. If you have made a purchase online, you may have added an extra digit and had an error message asking you to check your credit card number. This is most likely the MOD 10 check. The MOD 10 Check is discussed in detail in Chapter 31.

If you think about it, the need to authenticate a credit card number is not unique to the card-not-present space. It is a more pronounced issue for the card-not-present space, but the card-present world also has to do the same check. For example when a consumer comes to a store and hands the merchant a credit card, they really have no idea if it is valid credit card. Counterfeit cards are a serious problem in the industry, and credit card associations and issuers are constantly looking for new ways to prevent counterfeiting.

The difference between the card-present and card-not-present world is that in a store the consumer gives the merchant a credit card they can swipe through a card reader to perform the card authentication. Assuming the card is not damaged the machine can then check to make sure it is a real card and start the payment process. If it is damaged, or fake in some cases, it may not swipe and the merchant will have to key it in to get the process started.

But think about the card-not-present credit card transaction. You can ask for all kinds of information from the consumer, but you cannot swipe a card for them. They give you a number and say "this is my credit card number." But how do you know this is a valid credit card number? Valid means it potentially could be a credit card number, not just a random set of numbers they made up. Credit cards today have between 13 and 16 numbers, with 16 being the most used standard. Would your staff still try to process an order if the credit card number they got was 20 digits?

Authorization

Assuming the card number passed the card authentication check, now you need to find out from the card issuer if the consumer has enough money available to make the purchase. You do this by requesting an "authorization." When you do this your request goes through the acquiring bank to the issuing bank, where they are responsible for checking the consumer's credit card number for authorization.

In the card-not-present transaction when you request an authorization the request goes back to the issuing bank where they will see if the credit card account is an active account, if sufficient funds are available and, if you request it, and provide the address information, they will perform an "address verification." The address verification check provided in this process compares the billing address provided by the consumer with the billing address on record with the issuing bank. Address verification will be discussed in more detail in Chapter 10.

Some things to keep in mind about authorizations:

- **Authorizations commit funds only, no money exchanges hands.** With an authorization no money has exchanged hands, it has only been committed. For example, when you check into a hotel and they swipe your card when you arrive they are trying to get an authorization for what they estimate the total bill to be. This will commit that amount of money on the consumer's credit card to pay the merchant when the merchant processes a settlement transaction. The settlement transaction cannot be processed until the goods or services have been shipped to the consumer.

- **Authorizations are cumulative.** Every time a merchant requests an authorization on a card you are using up some of the consumer's credit line. If you make mistakes in your order process and re-run an authorization, you are committing more of the consumer's credit line. Likewise if you process an authorization for a consumer, and they cancel the order before a settlement is processed or goods are shipped, the authorization you processed does not go away unless you reverse it or it expires. Even though no payment will ever be made on these authorizations, the consumer's credit line can be gobbled up with these commitments and they will not be able to make any purchases until the authorizations expire or are reversed by the requesting merchant. Merchants that don't try to clean up these authorizations, or who process multiple authorizations on a consumer can cause another merchant to get a decline on an order when money is really available. This is a good way to piss-off a consumer, no one likes to get declined only to find out a store they went to screwed them up. For example a consumer with a credit line of $5,000.00 going in to purchase a new computer finds the one they like, and starts the checkout process. The clerk runs the authorization for $3,000.00 and gets an approval. Later that same day the consumer finds an even better deal with the same computer and a flat screen monitor from another merchant. The consumer decides they just have to have a new flat screen monitor to go with this new computer. So they call and cancel the original order and place a new order with the second merchant for $3,000. The original merchant hadn't shipped any goods yet, and simply canceled the order in their system. They don't process authorization reversals. When the issuing bank gets this request from the second merchant they will still have the other pending authorization for $3,000 and with new request for $3,000 the consumer is now at $6,000. The consumer looks like they are one grand over their limit, and the issuing bank will decline the authorization.

- **Authorizations expire on their own.** Authorizations don't last forever — they expire. The amount of time you have on an authorization may be different from card type to card type. Typically they last a week. If an authorization expires before you process a settlement you may have to process a re-authorization. A re-authorization is where you take an expired authorization and reprocess it to re-commit the funds.

- **The authorization must be the amount you expect to settle on.** When you request an authorization, by rule from the card associations you are supposed to be requesting an authorization of the amount you expect to settle on. If you get an authorization for $100 you cannot process a settlement of $500 against it. The amounts don't have to be exact — the association has built-in variances to account for industries like food service in which tips are added after an authorization is requested. These variances are percentage amounts over or under an authorization amount the bank will still process a settlement on.

Authorization Reversal

As you can see, you can get in trouble with authorizations under certain conditions, so a good tool to use is the "Authorization Reversal." The authorization reversal is what you would process when you are not going to process an order to settlement, in order to free up a consumer's credit line. Sounds great, right? Well the fact is most merchants don't use this process, as it can be complicated to integrate into their systems, and the number of times a consumer's credit line is tapped out by authorizations is generally rare because the authorizations do expire.

If you do implement authorization reversals, be aware that not all payment processing solutions, providers and/or issuers support this process. In short you could have this set up in your system and your payment processor could support this, but the consumer's issuing bank may not support it. In this case you are out of luck — the only way to get rid of this authorization is to let it expire or call the issuing bank directly.

More than likely you will never have to deal with this, but if you sell high dollar goods or services you better be prepared to deal with it.

Settlement

So the card is good, and the consumer has money, so how do you ask for your money? You do this by processing a settlement request. A settlement is where money actually changes hands. You request a settlement through your acquiring bank who pulls it from the issuing bank.

You typically cannot submit a settlement request for payment until you have shipped the goods or services to the consumer. So for orders that have split shipments, delayed shipments or backorders are in play, you have to wait to settle until you have shipped each of the goods.

Generally speaking if you deliver your goods or services electronically, such as software downloads, subscriptions or content viewing you can immediately request a settlement when you request the authorization. If you have physical products then you have to wait until the product is shipped to the consumer. In some cases, if your inventory is back-ordered or you are awaiting the products yourself, the authorization may expire before you can process the settlement. In these cases you will have to re-authorize the transactions prior to processing a settlement.

Credit

So what happens when the consumer returns the goods to you? You had processed an authorization and a settlement and the money has been handed over, and now you have to refund money back to the consumer. This is done by processing a credit. When you do this your acquiring bank will pass money back to the consumer's credit card.

When a consumer requests a refund, only refund back to the same method of payment they used to pay you originally. This is an easy scam from fraudsters to purchase goods with credit cards and request credits in cash.

Charge-backs & Represents

The final part of the money flow is not a merchant's favorite, and it has to do with what are called "charge-backs." Charge-backs are what occur when the consumer goes back through their issuing bank to say that they didn't place an order or they didn't get what they were supposed to get.

There are two general categories of charge-backs. Fraudulent charge-backs, in which the consumer says they did not place an order, and did not receive goods or services. Then you have "customer service charge-backs," in which the consumer admits they placed an order, but disputes the charges for any of a number of reasons such as, they didn't receive the goods or services, or they returned them to the merchant, or they didn't get what they ordered.

Charge-backs are coded by type, and each card association and acquiring bank is a little different on how they present them to a merchant. But the process is basically the same: they will present the charge-backs to the merchant with a request to "represent" the order with supporting documentation to prove the order was valid.

Remember from earlier in the book, I wrote that when it comes to who pays for fraud, the merchant does in the card-not-present space. One of the things that makes catching fraud so difficult is that charge-backs can take up to 90 days to be processed and sent back to a merchant. By that time a fraudster could have already maxed out a credit card at your site, if you are not doing anything to stop them.

The charge-back is coming from an issuing bank, and the "represent" request will be coming from a merchant going through the acquiring bank back to the issuing bank. When you "represent" an order you are trying to prove that the order was from the consumer who is disputing it and was completed in accordance with the association policies and procedures. In the card-present world a merchant would send a copy of a signed register receipt. In the card-not-present world there is no signed receipt. Here you are relying on the billing and shipping information provided and the signed delivery receipt, if you have one.

Charge-backs are nasty little *buggers*, as they have associated fees with processing them. In other words, every time a merchant gets a charge-back request from an issuing bank, they are charged a charge-back fee. Charge-backs and liability are discussed in greater detail in the next chapter.

Chapter 3

Charge-backs & Fraud Liability

In the previous chapter we introduced the concept of charge-backs. As you can see, no one is really excited about charge-backs. They were intended to provide a means for merchants, banks and consumers to resolve cases of abuse or fraud. They have been pretty good at doing this, but they have also created a lot of finger pointing and higher costs for everyone involved.

Let's refresh our memory when it comes to who is liable to pay for fraud. For fraud that occurs in the card-present world, the card association typically picks up the costs for fraud. However the merchant will still have some associated costs that are not covered by this. These include the costs to process an order, to handle the charge-back, the shipping costs, etc. The merchant will also have to pay a charge-back fee.

In the card-not-present world the merchant is typically the one paying for the fraud. They already paid and lost the goods, all of the overhead costs they spent on the order, and they will still have to pay a charge-back fee.

For customer-service charge-backs, the merchant pays a charge-back fee, and unless they can resolve the customer service issue they may have physical loss of goods and services and associated overhead costs.

Some merchants will go out of their way to resolve customer service complaints up front to prevent a charge-back fee. They create policies of refunds on disputes; they encourage customers to call the business if they aren't happy and they allow for refunds without returns. Why would a merchant do this? Well consider what is at stake. To the merchant their risk is the sum of the charge-back fees, the goods themselves, either lost or not returned, and the potential for increased basis points on their sales if their fraud losses get too high.

Charge-back Liability Example:

Total Sale = $100.00
Margin (22%) = $22.00
Credit Card Issuer Interchange & Acquirer MDR (3.5%) = $3.50

Net Profit = Margin - Credit Card Issuer Interchange & Acquirer MDR

The merchant will make $18.50 from this one sale, if it ends up as a charge-back, it will cost them:

Net Profit = $18.50
Consumer Refund = $100.00
Charge-back Fee = $25.00

Net Loss to Merchant = Net Profit -(Consumer Refund + Charge-back Fee)

The merchant will have lost $106.50 on this order. That means they would have to sell 4.8 more orders at this same amount just to make up this one loss. This example does not even take into account all of the merchant's costs, such as overhead and processing fees. It also assumes a very low charge-back fee — if they are doing e-commerce and are considered high risk, the charge-back fee could be $100 or more.

Charge-back fees are not fixed, they are different from bank to bank, and they also grow in cost depending on the number of charge-backs you have. If you have a significant problem with fraud you could find yourself paying higher charge-back fees than the actual cost of the goods sold.

How did this happen? As merchants tried to prevent abuse by consumers, they pushed disputes to the bank. The banks retaliated by increasing their fees. The card associations reacted to the increase in charge-backs by setting thresholds for the total percentage of orders that are charge-backs, along with the total percentage of dollars processed. If your charge-backs go above these thresholds you get hit with higher fines, and they keep going up until you get below the threshold. We call this the "going out of business plan" for the merchant. At the time of writing this book these thresholds were around 1% of total monthly transactions or 2.5% of total dollar volume. Beyond the charge-back fees, the number of charge-backs you have can effect the basis points you pay on each order. Merchants that exceed these limits are considered high risk. If they were considered high-risk they would have lost $181.50 on that same order and would now have to sell 8.25 orders of the same size to make up that one loss.

As you can see it is a scary proposition — one that has high stakes for the merchant. Merchants are very focused and motivated to control their losses to ensure that they don't get compounded by escalating charge-back fees.

BE FOREWARNED: *For Internet casinos, the U.S. card associations and issuing banks follow a policy that accepting a wager by a U.S. individual is in violation of federal law, and upon receiving a dispute from the cardholder, will immediately issue a charge-back.*

Business Case Study

ABC Electronics is evaluating the impact of charge-backs on their net profit. ABC Electronics is a $25 million dollar a year business with margins of 14%. The company is experiencing 5% charge-backs and the CEO has asked the CFO to explain the impact of charge-backs on the business, showing what the impact would be if they lowered it to 3% and what would happen if it increased further to 8%.

Assumptions			
Average Order Amount	$25	$25	$25
Orders	1,000,000	1,000,000	1,000,000
Charge-back Rate	3%	5%	8%
Impact on Operations			
Revenue	$25,000,000	$25,000,000	$25,000,000
Lost Goods	-645,000	-1,075,000	-1,720,000
Bank Refund to Cardholder	-750,000	-1,250,000	-2,000,000
Per Item Visa Fee (54% @ $100 per item)	-1,620,000	-2,700,000	-4,320,000
Per Item MC Fee (22% @ $100 per item)	-660,000	-1,100,000	-1,760,000
6 Month Visa High-risk Fee ($20K/month)	-120,000	-120,000	-120,000
6 Month MC High-risk Fee ($50K/month)	-300,000	-300,000	-300,000

Total Charge-back Impact	-4,095,000	-6,545,000	-10,220,000
Revenue Net Charge-back Fees	$20,905,000	$18,445,000	$14,780,000
Impact on Revenue	-16.4%	-26.2%	-40.0%
Operating Expense per Order	$14.94	$14.94	$14.94
Fraud Expenses per Order	$4.09	$6.56	$10.22
Margin	24%	14%	-.6%

Part II

Credit Card (Card-Not-Present) Fraud
How fraudsters steal from merchants

Why do fraudsters steal? To make money. So when a fraudster is stealing from a merchant it is their intent to make money. They may do this by directly reselling the goods or services they got from a merchant or by tricking a merchant into refunding cash or other monetary devices (gift cards) for goods or services that were theirs to begin with.

The fraudster is going to make themselves look and "feel" like they are someone else, and they are good at it!

In this section of the book we are going to dive deeper into understanding the fraudster. We are going to look at the history of fraudulent activity, the types of schemes they use, and ways to describe specific fraudster "personalities." To begin our discussion I want to segment fraudulent activity into four categories, Identity Theft, Social Engineering, Convenience (ease of use), and Internal Fraud.

These four categories give us a generic way to describe a fraudster's trick or scam by describing the activities and characteristics of the order the fraudster is presenting.

Category	Order Characteristics
Identity Theft	Large purchases, bust out activity (maxing out of cards in short time periods), many purchases, perfect identities, address, phone and Credit

	card data look clean.
Social Engineering	Attempting to find out information by asking questions, or to change information through social interaction. Hijack orders by changing shipping information, or changing billing data on an existing credit card account.
Convenience (Ease of Use)	Testing cards to see if they work by making small purchases at safe locations like gas stations, electronic download services, or fee-for-service locations.
Internal Fraud	Organized fraudulent activity by person or persons working in a company, sharing information on how to perpetrate fraud to conducting actual theft.

These four categories are just the beginning, as you read through this section you will get more specific descriptive discussions on schemes and fraudster personalities. The main reason I start with these four categories is to give you a starting context for describing fraudsters so you can start to tie historical fraud knowledge with types of schemes and personalities.

Why is it important that we describe and categorize fraudster activities? The main reason is it helps us detect patterns and develop fraud-prevention techniques to stop these types of fraudulent behaviors. In working in fraud prevention it is important to not only build strategies that can detect sophisticated fraud activity but that can also shut the door once you have spotted a fraud pattern. No fraud practitioner wants to be known as the one that could stop the most sophisticated fraudster, but let the dumb ones keep coming back for more. I say this because it is easy to focus so hard on one type of fraudster, one point of attack, that we lose sight of the bigger picture. Remember, fraud has always been around. The moment you successfully stop a fraudster's attack they will be looking for a new attack. Likewise, if you don't stop them, they will keep coming back until you do.

Take another look at the four general categories listed above. Where would you focus your attention to try and spot ("Spotting") this type of fraud activity? What would you do to shut the door and stop ("Stopping") that type of fraud from reoccurring? The following table shows some of the places you can look for these activities and how you could shut the door.

	Spotting	Stopping
Identity Theft	Large numbers of purchases to one address, unusual purchases like 4 cameras, 5 computers, multiple cards with same address, multiple accounts with one address	Check for multiple accounts, look at purchase patterns over 90 days, use out-of-pocket checks, cross-merchant checks
Social Engineering	Phone calls to CSR team or internal sales with questions about order process, order amounts, use of multiple cards for single purchase, attempts to update shipping of billing information. "I put in the wrong address on my order." "I am on the road, and need you to send it to my girlfriend or friend."	Reprocess all changes through normal risk-prevention processes, conduct a call back on all in-route address changes, or simply do not allow them
Convenience	Lots of cards with small purchase amounts, purchase of first item on the website or doesn't actually take delivery of goods or services	Use of velocity of change and velocity of use checks, hot lists
Internal Fraud	Systemic fraud, fraud ring appears to be hitting you, see fraudsters constantly coming in just under your thresholds, or you find a particular identity that seems to keep popping up every couple of weeks that should have been stopped but always seems to get through the process	Strong employment checks, education, accountability and checks and balances, no one person with the keys to the kingdom. Don't allow CSRs to override their own orders.

If this still doesn't make sense, don't worry. I will be discussing the schemes, personalities and fraud-prevention techniques in much more detail as we go through the book. The intent of this exercise is to share a mindset. When you read stories of fraudulent activity, or share stories with peers, put on your fraud practitioner hat and analyze the activities that let the fraudster gain access and commit fraud (spotting), and then think about how you would prevent that same fraudster from returning (stopping).

Chapter 4

History of Fraud Online

Fraud is not new. The taking of property from others has been around as long as man has been on this earth. Fraud is characterized as the taking of goods or services from another by use of trick or device.

In some cases the concept of fraud is very clear, such as cases in which a fraudster is clearly trying to pass off stolen credit cards or trying to steal goods going to another individual. But not all fraudsters are hardened criminals. In some cases what may look like a good consumer is actually nothing more than a fraudster. For example, a consumer may believe he or she is smarter than the merchant and will order a product with the intent of using it and returning it. Or a consumer may order goods, receive it, and say they didn't receive it. For some consumers, who are normally good consumers, they don't believe these types of activities are actually fraud. But to the merchant the end result is no different than if a hardened criminal had used a stolen credit card.

What motivates a fraudster to commit fraud? The money? The thrill or danger involved? Or is it the test of skill? It really doesn't matter, as the intent is what I am concerned with — the intent of taking goods or services by use of trick or device.

For a broad set of consumers and merchants, they correlate the rise in credit card fraud online with identity theft. In reality identity theft is one of the oldest schemes in the book. The fact is we are all just hearing more about it in the news today. It may seem that identity theft is a new phenomena of the Internet age, but in reality one of the best ways to disappear throughout the ages was to adopt a new identity. What better way to adopt a new identity then to steal it from another. No doubt, fraudsters can acquire a copy of a birth certificate and from that they can get a social security number and other documents to steal a consumer's identity. Identity theft is only a part of the problem — a single mechanism to commit fraud. Identity theft simply offers fraudsters another way to commit crimes and to hide them from detection.

How has the Internet Changed the Rules?

With the Internet, fraud scams are more efficient because you don't have to travel to physical stores, or potential marks, to test, or use, stolen credit cards. They are easier to hide because the fraudster is transparent — you don't see who you are doing business with, when doing business online. With the traditional Mail Order and Telephone Order channels, the level of transparency was pretty high, but merchants still had physical communication in telephone orders, and longer processing times in mail order, to work with. Additionally in the Telephone Order channel, if a Customer Service Representative was suspicious they could always ask more questions with the consumer on the line.

With the Internet the consumer and the fraudster can mask themselves by faking the data points they send to you, making it easier for them to abuse banks and businesses. With the Internet there is no live communication with a consumer. If the data looks suspicious you have to either reject the order outright, accept it with the risk of fraud or have someone investigate the order and try to get back in touch with the consumer — all very costly. Likewise consumers doing business online expect fast turnarounds on their orders.

How has Fraud Evolved?

Going back to the mid 1990's, we can see the beginning of real commerce from the Internet. I want to start our discussion here to show how, in a span of only ten years, so many different fraud scams evolved in order to give you a feel for the scope and pace of change.

With the start of e-commerce back in 1994 we started to see the first true buy buttons appear on the Internet. Not soon after we started to see several types of fraud. The first fraud trend to be seen was the use of "Famous Names" to commit fraud. In this attack the fraudster would use third-party stolen credit cards with the celebrity of the day's name.

In this attack you need to remember when you complete an authorization, the name used in the purchase is not checked. The fraudsters knew this and they used this to their advantage. They also knew human behavior: Businesses were excited about the Internet, "a whole new world" and they were too excited about the fact they got an order in the first place to actually think someone might be trying to steal from them. Likewise how many people actually check the names of each order to see if the name looks real?

It had to be a fun conversation, and an embarrassing moment for all, when they saw how many orders were being placed by Mickey Mouse, Bill Clinton, Lex Luther and John Wayne.

So merchants got smarter and they implemented rules to check the name being used. But it was only partially effective, as there are so many possible names, and so many people with the same name. Likewise the fraudsters moved on to new attacks.

Next came the technical attacks in which developers created card-generator applications that could come up with real credit card numbers, and they put them out on the Internet. Credit card generators were available everywhere for download on the Internet and fraudsters wasted no time using these generators to find credit card numbers they could use to make purchases.

These attacks were typically targeted at the same vendor, meaning a fraudster would focus their attacks on a single merchant to defraud them over and over again. As time progressed a new trend emerged in which the fraudsters start to jump from site to site, not staying long and hitting multiple merchants with fewer hits to make their activities less noticeable. This was very disturbing as most of the merchants at this time were relying on home-grown applications and manual reviews to prevent fraud. Merchants had no way to see cross-merchant activity until the card associations reported it and by then it was too late.

After 1996 fraudsters started to use the Internet as a test bed for stolen credit cards. Before the Internet, fraudsters used to take stolen cards to the local gas station where they could test to see if the card was still active and good by trying to buy a gallon of gas at the pump. If it worked they went on a shopping spree. The trend now is for fraudsters to use the Internet to test credit cards and then go on shopping sprees.

Up to this point the fraudsters were still relying on old tried-and-true techniques to get credit card information. They used skimming, dumpster diving, mail theft, actual theft of people's cards and application fraud. But as Internet commerce grew you started to see a group of fraudsters using the Internet to harvest credit card information. The fraudsters go out on the Internet to attack merchant sites and get new identities and card information to use to defraud the same, or other, merchants. These fraudsters use a technique called "cracking" as their main method to retrieve this data.

If the Internet boom was a creative boom, the fraudsters were right there with the industry. Groups of fraudsters found more and more clever ways to steal goods and services without the hassle of having to find actual credit cards, and trying to mask their identities. Fraudsters started to hijack orders. They would hack into merchant sites, or watch consumers, and find out what and when they placed an order so they could steal the shipment. The fraudster would either wait for the goods to arrive and take them at the point of delivery. Or they would call the merchant, or shipping company, and change the delivery address while it was in route. As the Internet began to peak in the late '90's, so did the fraudster's creativity in committing fraud.

As 1998 rolled around, the Internet is filled with e-commerce websites. Established merchants are climbing all over themselves to get online, and new merchants are trying to set up the next big retail conglomerate. Everyone is predicting the fall of the direct retail channels, and the rise of the e-commerce world. So what a better time for fraudsters to commit more sophisticated securities and property scams.

Fraudsters took this Internet fever and used it to their benefit by setting up dummy merchant sites where they could funnel credit cards through their own site to create cash flow and then before the charge-backs rolled in they would shut the doors and leave the country. In some cases the merchants would share credit card information with fraud rings to have them commit fraud at other sites.

Not too long after this we started to see the mass theft of identifies from the Internet through information that is provided online under the Freedom of Information Act. The most famous example of this was the mass theft of Military IDs from the Internet and then the follow on use of these identifies to steal from multiple merchants. Since then the private sector and government have become more careful about sharing this information. The problem for our government is the Freedom of Information Act, making a lot of this information public domain. But the sad fact remains that even if this information was not on the Internet, a fraudster can still go to state and county public offices to collect this type of data. Understanding this dilemma, merchants started to look for new ways to verify consumer information.

So merchants online started to think about ways they could stop fraud. One of the methods merchants developed was the use of consumer accounts. The merchant would set up a consumer account the first time the consumer tried to make a purchase. When the merchant set up the new account they would perform a series of checks to validate that the information the consumer provided was true. Merchants typically asked for more data from the consumer with this method, but they offered the consumer an easier "one-click" checkout process as an incentive to provide it. The concept was good, and consumers and merchants liked the new account method. This method was very popular at auction and larger e-commerce sites. But fraudsters liked this new method as well. Most merchants were only performing their fraud checks when an account was set up. Merchants weren't performing fraud checks when a consumer changes their shipping address, or added a new card. For fraudsters, they could set up new accounts with one credit card, and change the credit card information in their account as many times as they wanted to commit fraud. In a 90-day charge-back cycle they could process a lot of purchases with a lot of credit cards. Fraudsters could also take over a consumer's existing account and change the shipping address and place a number of orders.

As auction sites like eBay and uBid got popular, a lot of new fraud schemes arrived specifically targeted at this community. From selling bogus goods to misleading the consumer as to the type and condition of goods sold. The online auction fraudster had many more scams they could pull. From setting up a number of auctions and selling goods they don't really have, collecting the payments and then changing their identity, to using stolen credit cards to buy goods they sell on auction sites. Fraudsters could also use the buyer's credit card information to buy additional goods that they then could sell back to other consumers on the site.

After 2000 we really started to see organization in the fraud attacks. Online gangs and fraud rings start to emerge. From Asia to Nigeria to Russia we see a very systematic fashion of attacks coordinated to move goods from the site to a third party to fence and sell them.

We also saw the emergence of social engineering in which fraudsters become bolder in their attacks, taking the initiative to contact the issuing banks, the merchants and credit bureaus to complete their fraud. Even when flags are raised the fraudster will have taken initiatives to validate their identity enough to get the merchant to ship the actual goods.

This is only a snapshot of the fraud scams committed over the last ten years, and only focuses on the online aspect of the card-not-present transaction. The fact is Visa estimates online fraud to be approximately seven times that of fraud in the card-present world. Some independent analysts have the estimate as high as 12.

Chapter 4

While payment fraud in the card-present world has seen some declines over the last 20 years, it has risen steadily in the card-not-present world. Fraud is not going to just stop occurring. The initiatives by the card associations will help curb fraud, but as a merchant today you have to be prepared to fight this battle; and for some of you reading this, that battle may mean the survival of your business.

Chapter 5

Common Fraud Schemes

I have been working with merchants for years, and I am still amazed at the creativity fraudsters come up with to defraud merchants. These people aren't stupid, uneducated thugs. They are educated, crafty and patient.

If there is one thing I have learned from my experiences, I know that even if you wanted to, it is not realistic to think you can stop all fraud. There are just too many ways to create a perfect one-use identity. The resources, time, money and people I would have to put into place to catch these fraudsters just don't make sense.

But the good news is you don't have to catch the perfect one-use criminal. The majority of fraudsters out there are still using the basic scams to defraud merchants because there are still too many businesses that aren't doing anything to stop them.

The purpose of this chapter is to give you an understanding of some of the general schemes that are out there. With this understanding you can look at your businesses and craft strategies to prevent fraud that most closely represents the type of fraud scheme your site sees.

This chapter will also give you the insight to look at fraud patterns to spot fraud schemes as they are being perpetrated against you. Remember that to be effective at preventing fraud you have to be proactive in the design of your strategy. Don't just model your fraud strategies off what you have been hit with in the past, but look at your vertical market and see what other common fraud schemes may be pointed at you.

Where do those Fraudsters get the Credit Card Numbers?

Have you ever wondered where the fraudster gets their credit card information from? The fact is, lists of valid credit card numbers are available on the black market, with different prices for valid credit cards and credit cards with the card security numbers provided. Where do all of these cards come from? From several places.

The major point is from a scheme called skimming, in which card numbers are being harvested in common places like restaurants, bars, hotels, ATMs and airports. The fraudster places fake devices in these locations where an accomplice, or the entire staff unknowingly, is swiping each credit card that comes in. These numbers are then collected, and sometimes sold, to be used for fraudulent activity.

Credit card numbers can also come from fake applications for credit, identity theft, account takeovers and from valid unused account numbers. Since credit card numbers are allotted to issuers in blocks, fraudsters can methodically check each credit card number in a sequence by using a credit card generator to test a bank's credit card numbers. Of all of these methods, identity theft is the most worrisome. In cases of identity theft a fraudster can look and feel perfect to all but the most sophisticated fraud solutions.

One Hit – One Merchant & One Hit – Multiple Merchants

This is one of the more difficult types of fraud to detect and prevent. In this scheme a fraudster will acquire a credit card profile and will make a single purchase from your site. They will not reuse your site again, or if they do it will only occur after very long periods, greater than three months. They are making more than one purchase on the credit card itself, but it is at different vendors rather than multiple purchases from the same vendor. The fraudster will also typically be drawn to very highly fence-able goods: electronics, jewelry, mobile phones, computer goods and gift cards.

Number of Purchases: 1
Billing & Shipping Address: Typically different; the shipping address will typically be a drop point or abandoned point
Shipping Method: Express Shipping
Phone: Bogus, or the real consumer's number
Purchase Amount: High
Fraud-Prevention Techniques: High dollar amount rule with express shipping rule, reverse lookup address and phone, use of fraud screening that does cross-merchant velocity-of-use checking, card security schemes

Consumer-Perpetrated Fraud

This is a scheme in which the consumer or an accomplice of the consumer makes a purchase and then denies they made the purchase, or that they never received the goods or services. All of the data points will look good but the consumer will swear they did not make the purchase and did not receive the goods or services. They may also say they placed the order but never received the goods or services.

The consumer calls their issuing bank for the credit card and disputes the transaction for one of these reasons:

- Claim they never made the charge
- Claim their account was abused by someone else
- Claim they never received the services
- Claim that their spouse never made the transaction

If the consumer says they never placed an order, take a look at your past records to see if they have ever made a purchase from you before, and make sure you put them into at least a warm list to watch for them in the future.

Number of Purchases: 1 or more
Billing & Shipping Address: Typically the same; or if different, a real address with a real person
Phone: Real consumer's number
Purchase Amount: Any
Fraud-Prevention Techniques: Signature required on delivery, use of consumer authentication techniques, Verified by Visa, MasterCard SecureCode and out-of-pocket checks, hot lists and warm lists, card security schemes

Card Generator Fraud

In this scheme a fraudster is working a block of card numbers to find one or more that will work on a purchase. They are typically working a specific issuing bank's numbers. They will target smaller banks, and ones that are not up to date on the card types and solutions. For example they may not be up to date on AVS systems or real-time authorizations, or they may have set up automatic authorizations for certain amounts. The fraudster will find the banks meeting this criteria and find out their weakness and then attempt to hit all the credit numbers with the issuing bank's assigned credit card number range. Once the fraudster successfully receives an authorization from one of the credit card numbers they will make one or more purchases with it, from your business and from someone else's business if they can.

You can spot someone hitting you with a card generator by looking at the velocity of use and change characteristics of the orders. They will have to try the card multiple times, so you will see the same card with different expiration dates, you will see the same address with a lot of credit card numbers attempted against it.

The software for card generators is very widely available, so you will see activity from seasoned as well as "kiddie" fraudsters, trying it out. If you catch this activity occurring, look at the data being submitted and hot list any elements that were the same across all of the orders, like the e-mail address, shipping address and phone number.

Number of Purchases: 1 or more
Billing & Shipping Address: Typically different, the shipping address will typically be a drop point, abandoned point or temporary address
Phone: Bogus, or the real consumer's number
Purchase Amount: Any
Fraud-Prevention Techniques: Velocity of use, velocity of change, fraud screening

Consumer Satisfaction Fraud

You can please some of the people some of the time, but you cannot please all of the people all of the time...

What do you do about that annoying customer that keeps charging back their orders, when you know you have done what they asked. They may say, "You didn't send what I ordered," "It didn't arrive when you said it would," or "I changed my mind." The fact is charge-backs are expensive, and some customers, God bless them, you just can't afford to have as a customer.

We have all heard, or experienced, the customer who purchased something, used it and then returned it saying they just aren't happy with it. Merchants try to explain to consumers that they cannot take it back, because it's used...but they simply complain to their issuer and the merchant is stuck with the bill.

I don't have any magic answer on catching these consumers up front, if I did I would be a rich man, but there are things you can do to limit your exposure. First if you are selling goods or services under $50 you should consider a no-hassle return policy. Just take it back, don't mess with a charge-back unless you have an iron-clad case. In some cases the dollar value of a purchase makes fighting a charge-back a worthless proposition.

Second, implement a warm list or use your hot list and add this consumer to the list. I would recommend a two-strikes-you're-out policy. One charge-back or return of goods or services and you are put on the warm list, two charge-backs or returns and you're on the hot list. Make sure you review your warm list quarterly to see how many good purchases have occurred from these customers, if they have a good purchase in that same time period remove them from the list. However if the consumer actually did process a charge-back, wait for two good purchases before you take them off of the warm list. Remember the hot list automatically declines the order and the warm list automatically causes a review. You can read more about hot and warm lists in Chapter 27.

Number of Purchases: 1 or more
Billing & Shipping Address: Typically the same
Phone: Real consumer's number
Purchase Amount: Any
Fraud-Prevention Techniques: Hot lists, warm lists

Credit & Return Fraud

This scheme has slowed down dramatically in the USA as most merchants have already implemented polices to avoid this scheme, but it still is occurring in Europe and Asia.

The scheme happens in one of two forms. The first is where a fraudster working alone will come in and make purchases for goods and services and then will return the goods to have a credit given in cash.

The second form of this scheme is where the fraudster works with an accomplice. The fraudster makes purchases with the fraudulent credit cards and the accomplice returns them for cash.

In both schemes there may be some time between the purchase and credit. On return they may or may not have the receipt. They will commonly try to do returns when not having a receipt when it is common, like during holiday shopping seasons.

What does the scheme have to do with e-commerce and MOTO? If your business has a direct retail presence you could see some of this type of fraud as cross-channel fraud. With the emergence of e-commerce and the buy online and return in-store capabilities, the fraudster can use this scheme to move goods and funds.

With this scheme you have to be very conscious of patterns of charge-backs on items not typically found to be charge-backs. The fraudster can target safer purchases with this scheme because they intend to return them to get cash or gift cards to then make purchases of higher end goods that they can sell on the street easier.

Most merchants in the U.S. have adopted a policy of only giving credits to the same credit card that was used for the purchase, or in the case of gifts they will give a gift card. This has curbed the scheme pretty well, but there is still a susceptibility to this scheme for most merchants because of the ability to make the fraudulent purchases, make the returns and then purchase another item.

Beyond adopting better return policies you can implement velocity of use and change checks on your credits and returns to catch people who are doing a lot of credits from a lot of different points. Be careful with this — make sure you know your customers. Some of your customers could very well have multiple people making purchases for them at the same store, and they could be looking to consolidate gifts and buy something different.

Number of Purchases: More than one
Billing & Shipping Address: Typically different, the shipping address will typically be a drop point or abandoned point
Phone: Bogus, or the real consumer's number
Purchase Amount: Any
Fraud-Prevention Techniques: Better return policies, velocity of change and velocity of use

Morphing Fraud – Repeat Offenders

In short the morphing attack is where a fraudster is hitting a single merchant multiple times using slightly different data points each time. These attacks are typically of short duration with multiple purchases being made and sent to the same address or within a very close proximity. The fraudster may change every data point except one or two, so you have to be doing some good cross-reference checking to catch them.

This scheme has a couple of different variations. I call them the "bust-out," the "slow morph" and the "multiple personality."

In the bust-out variation the fraudster will make multiple purchases from your site within a short timeframe with a number of different credit cards. All of the goods and/or services will be going to the same location, but all of the other data may change between purchases.

In the slow morph attack, the fraudster will make purchases over time with elapsed time between purchases to prevent raising any flags, and will change the credit card, address and phone slowly over time, just keeping in front of you.

In the multiple personality attack, the fraudster will set up several different personas with different cards and make periodic purchases over a 30 to 90-day timeframe. I have seen cases where the morphing attack was pulled off with 2 to 3 hits per month, all spread out over a 90-day period. The fraudster used three different credit cards and personas and made one purchase with each persona per month for a three-month period and then disappeared. The merchant in this case was using velocity of use and change, but was only counting usage and change for a 24-hour period to attempt to catch bust-outs. They finally caught on when they starting doing some research on past charge-backs to see the fraudster was using variations of the same name. For example "Sara, Sarah, Sam, Samantha, Bill, Bob, William, Willard and Wilda."

The morphing attack is a little easier to spot if you have good velocity of use and change checks in place. The problem is determining how many purchases or changes constitute actual morphing. As a merchant we all pretty much assume and want to have our customers come back and buy from us. We never assume the fraudster knows this as well, and will play us based on this. Making a purchase once a month for three months wouldn't in itself set off any alarms, but what they are buying and how the data points they send us change does.

In looking at catching morphing attacks you will have to really think about how you can look at previous account activity, and how you can look at the products purchased as well. The velocity of change and use checks are the best mechanisms to catch someone morphing their identity in their attack.

Some of the things you can look for to catch these morphing fraudsters include:

- Look at the typical buying patterns for your merchandise. Would someone typically buy the product sold more than once in a day, week, month or year? For example if you sell televisions online, how often would the same person buy another television on the same day, week or month? If you sell jewelry, how often does someone buy the exact same piece of jewelry in a day, week, month or year?
- If you are already looking at velocity of change and use on a daily basis today to stop bust-outs, don't change it. Add another combined look at velocity of use and change over a 6-month period

in which you look at the number of purchases on a given credit card, e-mail, phone and address. And track the number of changes of a credit card number to an e-mail, phone and address.

- Look at the name associated with a credit number to see how many times it is changing. The name is typically not a good tool for doing fraud checks, but in the morphing attack, the attacker can change the name with everything else being the same. They don't always do this. Though in the case I discussed earlier the fraudster used the same name, which is how we caught him, and stopped him from starting back up the following month with a fresh set of cards.
- If you are doing e-commerce, track the IP address being used by the fraudster and to check it against the IP address from past charge-backs to see if they are coming from the same points. It is very rare that they will have the same IP address, this typically means a real novice fraudster, but you can see trends to certain proxies or regions.

Number of Purchases: More than one
Billing & Shipping Address: Typically different, the shipping address will typically be a drop point or abandoned point
Phone: Bogus, or the real consumer's number
Purchase Amount: Any
Fraud-Prevention Techniques: Velocity of use, velocity of change, geolocation, and consumer authentication, hot lists, card security schemes

Fraud Rings

Nothing strikes fear in a merchant's heart like the dreaded fraud ring. If you are lucky you have only read about them in the paper or seen a piece on them in the news. If you're not lucky, you have experienced how devastating they can be.

Fraud rings are very good at finding the weak points in your fraud-prevention process and exploiting them quickly and efficiently. They are patient, taking a lot of time to learn about your policies and procedures. They typically perpetrate one or more of the other fraud schemes listed above to find out how you react before they make a more massive attack.

- They will target a merchant and see what channels and purchase instruments they will accept

- They will research the company via social engineering to see how the business operations work, how data is stored, how long before charge-backs occur
- They will look for vulnerability in the site, like dollar thresholds, and rules that are applied
- They will attempt to hack the site

What are fraud rings looking for? They want to find out where you really start looking at orders. Are there dollar thresholds you use that you don't do any fraud screening on below certain amounts? Do you use any manual reviews; follow up with phone calls or reverse look-ups? Do you use hot lists, or fraud screening solutions? Each of these gives them a different angle of attack and tells them how to attack. These things also tell them what pace they can attack a merchant at. They will also look at how you change across time — do you have more lenient policies during slow times, or during peak holiday times?

One of the favorite times for a fraud ring to hit is during the Christmas season because they know you can't look at everything, and you probably have temporary help in that is not as experienced. They also know you can't take down your systems without effecting the rest of your business. Fraud Rings aren't typically greedy about their attacks and will patiently attack your site during a holiday season to take you for a reasonable sum before the holiday season is over. They will be long gone before you can really see what was happening.

In stopping fraud rings, you have to focus on the basics of preventing fraud. The most basic point for fraud rings is catching the similar or common data points that can help you isolate the fraud ring and attempt to stop them. Using tools like geolocation, freight forwarder lists, delivery address verification, consumer authentication, and velocity checks, you can isolate these common data points. The most common data points you should be looking for are the use of the same address, phone or e-mail accounts. Or very close similarities between them (e.g., 12 Main Ave, 12a Main Ave, 12b Main Ave).

In the cases where the fraud ring is hitting multiple sites in their attack, use of the freight forwarder and fraud-screening techniques that do cross-merchant velocity checks will help in catching these fraudsters. A lot of the fraud rings will use freight forwarders to move the goods out of the country to places such as Asia, Eastern Europe, Africa and South America.

The more dangerous fraud rings are typically well thought out, using true account takeovers with long active periods of good purchasing behavior in which everything will look OK, before performing a bust-out. You also have to assume they have plenty of valid credit card numbers to use since most are associated with skimming or harvesting activities for valid credit card numbers. There are very well known fraud rings that operate out of Eastern Europe and Africa. If you check out the United States Governmental sites for the Secret Service and Federal Trade Commission you can usually find advisories about these groups. The only point about checking out these sites, is once you see them in print, you have probably already been de-frauded.

Number of Purchases: More than one
Billing & Shipping Address: Typically different, the shipping address will typically be a drop point or abandoned point
Phone: Bogus, or disposable mobile phone number
Purchase Amount: Any
Fraud-Prevention Techniques: Velocity of use, velocity of change, geolocation, consumer authentication, hot lists, fraud screening, freight forwarder, rules engines, card security schemes

Collusive Fraud — Internal Fraud

Collusive fraud is when a member of the merchant's staff is working with the fraudster. This person could be directly helping the fraudster commit the acts, or could be funneling goods to them.

The most common version of this type of fraud is where the inside person will work in a merchant's call center to learn the fraud prevention policies and procedures. The inside person then feeds this information to the fraudster in a form in which they can get around your current fraud policies.

Other variations of this scheme are where the staff member is actually putting in orders or changing shipping information to have goods sent to other points. Or they are taking down credit card and personal information of consumers and then using this to make other purchases there or at other merchants.

Number of Purchases: More than one
Billing & Shipping Address: Same or different
Phone: Disposable mobile phone number or real consumer's number (not the fraudsters)
Purchase Amount: Any, but usually more on the upper end

Fraud-Prevention Techniques: Velocity of use, velocity of change, hot lists, fraud screening, rules engines, implementing tiered reviews with managers reviewing staff and making sure you document the name of the staff member who works on each transaction

Identity Theft

Identity theft is a major issue in the marketplace with a case of identity theft being reported every 79 seconds in 2001, according to MasterCard Risk Symposium. The United States Federal Trade Commission (FTC) estimates about 700,000 cases of identity theft per year. The United States Postal Service puts the number around 500,000 and Security Management Magazine August 2002 estimated 500,000 as well. In Canada 6,188 cases of identity theft were reported last year.

In the United States the FTC has been charged with tracking cases of identity theft through the Federal Trade Commission Identity Theft Clearinghouse. In Canada cases of identity theft are tracked through the credit bureaus.

Every day in the United States 3,100 people are victims of identity theft and this has been like that for the last 12 years with a slight increase in the past couple of years. The United States Postal Service reported it will typically take a victim 14 months before they find out their identity has been stolen, and it will take these victims an average of 175 hours to clear their name.

As you can see identity theft is a major issue. The fact is a lot of merchants and consumers believe that the Internet is somehow to blame for the rise of identity theft, but in reality the Internet is not even in the top ten for methods of acquiring identity takeover information. Database intrusion was the number one method for stealing data followed by dumpster diving. Once a fraudster steals someone's identity what do they do with it? According to the FTC 42% is used for credit card fraud, 20% for utility fraud and 13% for bank fraud.

Fraudsters can very easily takeover and create new identities. The CDC puts out an annual book that can tell the layman how to obtain birth certificates on anyone. The birth certificate is bar-none the best breeder document for identity theft. So where do they get the basic information on a person to start this process? From dumpster diving, database cracking and car rental agencies to name a few. Anywhere you might have to fill out an application.

As of 2002 all 50 states delineated identity theft as a crime, whereas before some states would have to use impersonation, check fraud, etc. to prosecute. California recently passed legislation CA Code 530.8 in the Penal Code stating that when someone reports this type of fraud banks must allow the consumer or police to have access to all records including the files on the application or changes to applications.

So what can you do about identity theft? First educate your customer service representatives on the tactics of fraudsters. Perform comprehensive customer validation, namely out-of-pocket checks. Also perform velocity of use and change checks and use third-party fraud screening that combines velocity across merchants.

If you have a case of fraud and a consumer calls you and says he or she is a victim of identity theft, be patient with the consumer. It may be true that he or she is a fraudster trying to social engineer you, but you should be polite and assume it really is a case of identity theft unless you have clear evidence to the contrary. Tell the victim they need to provide you with and an affidavit and police report, with the police report number and officer's phone number on it. The consumer can get a sample affidavit from the FTC website or they can get an identity theft reporting kit from our website at www.fraudpractice.com. One note on the affidavit, technically the affidavit does not have to be signed or notarized to be legal, but ask for this anyway, if nothing else it is forensic evidence and could be used as evidence of perjury.

Chapter 6

Identifying the Fraudsters

With all of the news on break-ins, stolen information, fraud and abuse, how do you make sense of all of the different characterizations of fraudsters? Hackers, crackers, Phreaks and Hactivists — it sounds like a bad horror movie. But there are some good reasons to understand what these terms mean.

First you get a feeling for the motivation of your fraudster. Find out why they are committing fraud. You also get a feel for how likely they will be to repeat their crime; or if it will mean others will repeat the crime. Finally you get an understanding of the tools and places where they get information on how to infiltrate your site and commit fraud.

The following short business case describes each of the fraudster characterizations. The intent is to give you a high-level view of the motive and potential activity of a particular fraudster characterization. Actual fraudsters could do more or less than the example I give. The examples are not intended to be all-inclusive, but should provide a good reference point.

Business Case – All Electronics, Fraudster Characteristics

ABC Electronics is a well-known electronics retailer with over 1,200 direct retail stores in 9 different countries (the United States, Canada, the United Kingdom, Ireland, Germany, France, Sweden, Italy, and their newest stores in China). ABC Electronics also has very active channels in mail order, telephone order and e-commerce, with 20% of their overall revenue coming from these non-direct channels.

While their roots in providing businesses with their computer and office automation equipment has always been the majority of the mail and telephone order sales they receive, approximately 18% of their non direct business comes from MOTO, their web business has been growing at a phenomenal rate of over 500% per year. Currently they receive other 1,000 orders per day from their web business.

ABC Electronics was a little rushed when they implemented their website and they didn't have the time to implement real-time payment processing. They decided to store the order information from their customers and process it in a batch during non-peak hours. ABC Electronics relies on a staff of four fraud reviewers residing in their call center to review all e-commerce and MOTO orders for fraud. Since their web-based business was not really a significant amount of the overall revenue, the web-based orders were typically the last ones to be reviewed, if they were reviewed at all.

Fraudster Type	Motivation	Potential Activity
Hacker	Prove technical prowess	The Hacker may attempt to see if they can access credit card data. If they can they may add an order or pull a list of orders from your system, which may include personal data and credit card information of consumers.
Cracker	Make money, steal anything possible	The Cracker will directly attempt to put in orders, or to pull out the credit card data to use for fraudulent activity.
Phreak	Make money, steal phone-related products	The Phreak would be the fraudster attempting to steal the company's prepaid mobile phones and their calling cards.
Hactivist	Make a statement	The Hactivist is the individual that will gain access to your systems to plant a virus to protest your newest stores in China, in order to protest human rights conditions.
Script Kiddie	Excitement, make money	The Script Kiddies are the ones attempting to use freeware card generators to make purchases on the website.
Criminal Gang	Make money, their business	The criminal gang would be working orders against the unprotected website
White Collar	Greed, make money	Would be providing individuals or gangs the information about the website being unprotected

Hackers

Hackers are individuals that attempt to gain access to computer systems and websites of businesses or individuals to be able to say they can do it and prove it to their peers. The activity of a hacker is not designed to steal or de-fraud an organization, but instead to prove the hacker's technical skills.

Hackers will typically leave a calling card in the systems they hack to prove to others they have been there, by leaving a piece of code, or taking a key piece of information meant to prove the hack was successful. Hackers want publicity – that is why they are doing it. They are not necessarily looking for tons of publicity, news and such, but there is a hierarchy of hackers, and they need to publicize their hacks to move up in that hierarchy.

On the websites dedicated to hacking you can see this hierarchy, and how hackers have to contribute to gain entry into the society. They have to show proof of ability. There are a number of these sites out there such as 2600, PHRACK (Phreaking & Hacking) and WAREZ. And there are a number of magazines dedicated to hacking. Hackers use tools called "warez" which are tools and devices they have developed to infiltrate websites. The fact is the tools for hacking a site are easily available on the Internet, and if your site is hacked you had better fix the holes they have shown you, or else others will try the hack as well.

The hacker is not someone you should focus on in preventing fraud. The folks in your IT Department, responsible for information security, should be focused on stopping hackers. The hacker is not the one who will commit fraud on your site, but the information they gain may be used by others to de-fraud you.

The hacker is someone who may attempt to see if they can access credit card information, a hot thing in the news these days. If they can, they may add an order or pull a list of orders from your system, which may include personal data and credit card information of consumers. They would post parts of this information to prove they had gotten in. With this information posted on a hacker website, a potential fraudster could find holes into a merchant's or bank's systems to pull all of the personal information, including credit card data, to use for fraudulent activity. They could also find hacks in systems to get in and learn your fraud-prevention processes.

One last note about hackers and the hacking community. If you get the "itch" to check out their sites, make sure you take strong virus and security precautions as these sites are notorious for downloading items on your computer just by visiting them. These little "gifts" they leave behind can collect data residing on your computer, learn your passwords or even take over a camera that may be attached to your computer, in which the fraudster can sit and watch everything you are doing.

Crackers

Crackers are individuals attempting to gain access to a website or system with the intent of using that activity to steal from the business or individual. They are not trying to prove anything. They don't want publicity. They want money, goods or information you have.

The cracker is a fraudster, and is an individual that both you and your IT information security personnel should be focused on. These individuals are using the same sites and materials as the hackers, but have crossed the line from proving their ability to attempting to profit from it.

Phreaks

Phreaks are crackers with a major in telephone, cell phone and calling card fraud. Their intent is to steal telephone time, and to use it or sell it on the street. Phreaks focus on sites that sell telephone, cell phone and calling cards. They will target these products and will attempt to move as much of it as they can in as short of a time frame as possible.

Phreaks are very focused on certain product types. Some phreaks will stand in public places and memorize people's calling card numbers to resell on the street. Other phreaks set up fake identities to purchase mobile phones they use or sell on the street. Still other phreaks focus on stealing pre-paid mobile phones and extra minutes. You may have seen these individuals in big cities selling cell phones, all ready for use, with super low charges. Or on one of the auction websites selling calling cards and prepaid mobile phones. You would be amazed at just how much telephone time is stolen annually by phreaks.

Hactivists

Think of a hacker with an agenda. These folks are the political activists of the fraudsters. They will attempt to hack or crack under the guise that they are serving a higher cause, and they feel this act is a justifiable means of protest. There are plenty of causes to go around, from stopping fur, animal-tested cosmetics, cigarette sales, use of oil, saving the environment and simply protesting the government.

The hactivist will gain access to a site or system with the firm intent of malicious activity. Whether they personally profit from the act is not of general importance to them. These are the ones that may not just steal from you, which is typically not their style, but they will put in a nice tasty virus to shut you down.

Script Kiddies

Script Kiddies are your casual fraudsters. They are not hardened fraudsters, and although the idea of potentially pulling off a fraud and profiting from it is nice, they are also motivated by the excitement of doing the theft.

The Script Kiddie may be a teenager, college student or highly technical individual who finds out about a tool or method to commit fraud and actually attempts to use it. The Script Kiddie is not a sophisticated criminal. They will be using tools and methods that are highly published, like card generators. They are typically easy to see and stop in your fraud-prevention strategies. Threats of prosecution, use of third-party branding that shows additional fraud checking, and fake information gathering (such as gathering the card security number, but not checking it) are typically enough to scare them off.

Criminal Gangs

The criminal gang is an organized group who intend to steal money, goods or services from one or more merchants. The criminal gang has multiple people involved in their scheme and will put as much effort into hiding their activity as they do in actually committing the fraud.

The criminal gang thinks big. They aren't really likely to be the ones trying to steal consumer data from your systems, they are the ones using stolen consumer data from skimming to move product from your site. They will set up drop points and fake addresses for coordinated thefts at multiple merchants all going to a single address, which will disappear the next day. They may also use freight forwarders to move product out of the country.

Audacity is a word I would use to describe the criminal gang. One of the scams pulled off by an organized criminal ring was the collection of consumer debit and ATM card numbers and PINS. The gang created realistic-looking ATM machines. They went out to stores with ATM machines and replaced them with the fake ones, which would collect the ATM card information and PINS. The ATM machine would tell the consumer the network is down and the consumer would wander off. The next day they came back and replaced the old machine. Then they harvested the numbers and started to withdrawal money from the ATM cards.

Another excellent scam pulled off by criminal gangs is the set up of fake websites that have the exact same look and feel as a real website in which they can collect logons and passwords. The gang sets up a fake website with the same web address as the real website, with a one letter difference that will pull up a website that looks exactly the same, and then collect the logon and password information and break into the accounts to send themselves money or steal credit card data. There was a very well publicized case of this with PayPal in which the gangs set up websites like www.paypalnet.com, www.paypal.com, and www.paypalsecure.com.

White-Collar Criminals

White-collar criminals are those individuals that attempt to de-fraud a business from the inside. These individuals are motivated by greed and money, and they exploit inside information, and/or access, to personally profit. The white-collar criminal could be working with external fraudsters, gangs, or individuals. There are many different definitions for white-collar crime, but for the purposes of card-not-present fraud, I label white-collar criminals as either active or passive.

The active white-collar criminal is one that directly attempts to steal consumer data to process fraudulent orders against that business or other businesses. They may directly place orders into the system, or monitor and accept orders that they know are fraudulent.

The passive white-collar criminals are the ones that pass on information about the policies and procedures to external personnel so they can commit the fraud. They are paid from the other criminals but they are feeding the information they need to stay under the radar screen of the fraud-prevention activities of the merchant.

Chapter 7

Reporting Fraud

So what do you do once fraud has occurred? As a merchant, who do you contact to report the crime? How do you try to prove your case to the issuing bank?

When you find that a fraudulent transaction has occurred you can report it in several ways. One of the ways is to use an online resource called the Internet Fraud Complaint Center (IFCC). The IFCC is a partnership between the Federal Bureau of Investigation (FBI) and the National White Collar Crime Center (NW3C).

The IFCC's mission is to address fraud committed over the Internet. For victims of Internet fraud, IFCC provides a convenient and easy-to-use reporting mechanism that alerts authorities of a suspected criminal or civil violation. For law enforcement and regulatory agencies at all levels, IFCC offers a central repository for complaints related to Internet fraud, works to quantify fraud patterns, and provides timely statistical data of current fraud trends.

What To Do If You Are Suspicious

If you are suspicious about an order, try to verify the transaction by asking the customer for additional information. These requests should be made in a conversational tone so as not to arouse the customer's suspicions. If the customer balks or asks why the information is needed, simply say that you are trying to protect cardholders from the high cost of fraud.

If you are on the phone with the consumer, put them on hold and call your acquiring bank for a Code 10 authorization. A separate phone call to your authorization center asking for a Code 10 authorization lets the center know you have concerns about a transaction. Ask for the name of the financial institution on the front of the card. Separately confirm the order with the customer. Send a note to his/her billing address, rather than the "ship to" address. On shipping the goods make sure you ship them with a signature required.

For addresses in which goods have been shipped and stolen, report it to the postal inspector at the United Sates Postal Service, in the area the fraud has occurred. This is important as they track fraud by address, and may have had other reports for the same address. They may implement a sting operation and/or be able to help you in a prosecution.

For large cases, contact your local police, FBI or Secret Service resources to see about pursuing potential investigation. Don't be surprised if your local law enforcement agency doesn't jump in to help you. There are a lot of cases of fraud, and unless you have a substantial loss or proof of a larger ring that would catch the attention of broader investigations, they won't be willing to get involved. Even if they find the culprit, unless the dollars involved are substantial, pursuing a prosecution may be difficult.

Chapter 8

Understanding the Law and Fraud Prevention

In developing your fraud-prevention strategy, make sure you consult with your Legal Department about what information you collect, store and use to prevent fraud. Likewise make sure you have a clear understanding of how you need to word your responses back to the consumer to make sure you don't have to meet other reporting and legal requirements for notifying the consumer.

So what legislation and legal points should you be following as a fraud practitioner? First and foremost make sure you understand the ins and outs of consumer data protection. From legislation such as the European Union Privacy Directive on Protection of Personal Data (EUPDPP) to privacy policies and appropriate use policies, what you do with consumer data can leave you open to very large lawsuits. Likewise make sure you understand how the Fair Credit Reporting Act (FCRA) and the Homeland Security Act apply to your vertical market and sales channels.

Fair Credit Reporting Act (FCRA)

FCRA mandates that agencies that are granting credit to a consumer and decide not to grant credit must send notice to the consumer of adverse action. FCRA was originally designed to help consumers understand why they weren't approved for mortgages. The focus of FCRA was to explain to consumers the points of credit worthiness that were used in consideration of a loan, and why the credit was not granted.

The fact you decide not to sell someone something because you suspect fraud does not mean you have to send notice or have to follow FCRA. But if you word your denial in such a way that indicates or sounds to the consumer that you are denying them credit, you could be held liable under FCRA. If you are granting credit in any form (such as credit cards, same as cash), you should be prepared to meet FCRA requirements.

European Union Privacy Directive on Protection of Personal Data

The European Union Privacy Directive is actually a framework for legislation directing member countries to act upon the framework to state specific country requirements for obtaining consent from consumers on the use and storage of any personal data.

This directive has led to the implementation of country-specific acts, such as the United Kingdom Data Protection Act of 1998. The main point you need to remember about these acts is that each country will have different requirements on how you maintain and secure data associated with consumers from their countries. Privacy is the key concern of these acts.

If you are doing business internationally, make sure you check with your Legal Department about specific requirements for the countries you do business in.

Consumer Data Protection Requirements

There are a number of pieces of legislation out there about handling consumer data and how you have keep it secure as a merchant. Your Legal Department is the best place to find specific guidance. Saying that, remember that all of this legislation is dynamic and could change at any time. For example the McCain Legislation defines data handling and consumer redress mechanisms, exceptions for fraud checks and would override FCRA, but could be years before it is enacted.

The Federal Trade Commission, using existing statutes such as, "safe Harbor" for Internet companies, state that "if you have a policy, disclose what you do with data, and comply with your stated policy" and if you do this you're OK. If you don't disclose what you do, or do something you've stated you don't do, you're subject to federal prosecution.

Under statutes, such as the Unfair Trade Practices Act, you will find that you need to notify consumers what will happen with the data obtained in the purchase activity.

The issue of protecting consumer data is directly related to concerns of online privacy. Online privacy can be defined as a customer's expectation that their online activities, transactions and preferences will be kept private, not used, misused or misrepresented, or otherwise used in unacceptable ways.

Consumers, government and businesses are concerned about the use of personal data. These concerns are the driving force behind the calls for legislation to protect this information. This, in turn, broadens the implications for businesses and scares consumers about fears of identity theft and too much government control.

The government is responding to the people, businesses are worried about implications for expanding e-commerce business and that leaves us all in a quandary. The Internet is not owned by any one country. The laws enacted by one country can affect merchants from other countries, so who has jurisdiction? Who do you call if you have a problem?

In a survey done by Harris/Westin in 1998 over 90% of the consumers surveyed were "concerned" or "very concerned" about threats to privacy. 60% of those surveyed wanted laws to govern how information was used on the Internet and 70% would favor industry efforts over regulation if companies and associations could implement effective practices.

Even with this overwhelming concern, each of us everyday agree to give up some of our privacy by trading information online in order to get some other information or service. From registering to view articles, to giving age and habit data to see our horoscope, we all make choices. In most of these cases our intent with sharing information is to get a more personalized experience on the web.

The promise of easier searches, simplified purchasing, free "stuff" and group buying power seem to lure us in. But what are these merchants and businesses doing with our personal data? Just how safe is it? Consumers are scared about identity theft, and they are scared about losing their transparency online as well. Who can blame them with the stories in the news and papers today? No one wants to live in a society that is watched 24x7 by Big Brother, but they also don't want to be a victim.

The fastest way to lose revenue is to not take consumer privacy seriously. No amount of marketing, attractive pricing or convenience will entice a consumer to conduct business online or offline if they believe that in conducting that business, their personal information will be compromised.

If you do any business online today you will see that the use of a Privacy Policy is now the norm. This has not always been the case. As consumer awareness heightened with big stories on thefts of card data, business awareness also increased to make sure they were doing things to ease that consumer concern. Over the last ten years there have been a lot of third-party organizations that have entered the scene to attempt to enforce privacy policies, such as TRUSTe, BBBOnline and others.

Businesses today are not just concerned with soothing consumer concerns to keep them coming back, but they are also concerned about their ability to use consumer information in fraud prevention and investigations of crime. They are also concerned about the repercussions of using that data: In using it will it leave them open to future litigation? Will it instigate hacking attacks or spur some type of governmental investigations? None of these activities are good for business.

Consumers and businesses must work together to make protection of consumer data and conducting business. As a business today provide your consumer with choices, and as a consumer take the time to understand what you are agreeing to when you are exploring the web. We all need to hope that government will take a slow and deliberate path on any sweeping legislation to allow the new commerce channels, such as eConsumer, to grow up.

As for our law enforcement community, they will have to catch up and set up new techniques to combat the growing fraud issues with e-commerce, and all of us as merchants doing business online must be proactive in using the data we do collect to try to prevent fraud and abuse. Those businesses that don't take this step won't be around for long.

Part III

Fraud-Prevention Techniques
32 of the most used fraud-prevention techniques

Rules, strategies, business processes, checklists, weights, techniques, tools, tests, modules, applets, policies, procedures, queries, lookups, investigations, reviews, requests, confirmations, qualifications, audits, compliance, verifications, quality assurance and quality control. It seems everyone has their own vocabulary and language to talk about how they prevent fraud.

I am not trying to define an official fraud practitioner "speak" in this book, but I want to take a little time to define some concepts so everyone understands context. In working with your peers, don't get stuck on what everyone calls a solution, technique or process, instead focus on what it does. I have had more titles than I can remember, and have had to explain my role and duties to customers on more than one occasion, but I didn't take it personally.

I like to keep my conceptual planning simple — the simpler the better. This is important because if your staff and peers can't understand what you are talking about when you walk them through it, you probably need to rethink how you are presenting it. I have found in some extreme cases that the conceptualizations and processes put into place at a business were so complicated it would take over a week with people from multiple departments just to decipher what was actually being done. This does not instill confidence in your management, and it could cost you valuable time in spotting a fraud trend.

There are two major concepts you need to be familiar with: "Fraud-Prevention Strategies" and "Fraud-Prevention Techniques." Strategies consist of business process and fraud-prevention techniques. A strategy is intended to manage fraud losses while keeping administration costs and sales conversion at acceptable levels. A technique is intended to check for a specific condition in an order and to prevent an order from processing if it passes or fails that check. A technique can be used to validate positive or negative conditions, and can be either interrogatory or descriptive.

To illustrate the two concepts and how they work together, I will use an example that most of us have thought about. Most of us have a retirement strategy. We state that we want to have a certain amount of money by the time we reach a certain age so we can retire comfortably. Now there are a lot of different ways we could attempt to reach this goal, we could put money into a 401k, IRA, stocks, bonds, certificates of deposit or lottery tickets. Each of these is a technique for investing, and provides different potential returns with varying degrees of risk. Our strategy has to take into consideration our age, our comfort with risk and our day-to-day needs to survive.

Creating a fraud-prevention strategy is not that different. You have to understand the goals of your business and weigh the value of each technique you implement to understand the associated costs and implications to administration costs, fraud reduction and potentially lost revenue.

In this section we focus on the fraud-prevention techniques. At the end of this section you should be able to understand what they are, how they work and what fraud they can stop. Fraud-prevention techniques are the building blocks of your fraud-prevention strategy, and your strategy will only be as strong as your understanding of their use.

Chapter 9

Fundamentals — The Anatomy of a Strategy

In this chapter I will discuss some basics of strategy design to get you started. Again the goal of this book was to give you an understanding of the fundamentals of credit card fraud-prevention techniques, and it does not go into extensive detail on designing an effective fraud-prevention strategy.

Saying that, lets talk about the basics of strategy design. There are five major phases of a strategy: Pre-screen, Payment, Post-screen, Review and Accounting. Each phase has distinct goals and techniques that can be used to accomplish those goals.

Phase	Activities
Pre-Screen	Hot Lists
	Positive Lists
	Velocity of Change
	Velocity of Use
	Rules
	Consumer Authentication
	Verified by Visa
	MasterCard SecureCode
Payment	Authorization
	Address Verification Service
	Advanced Address Verification
	ACH (electronic checking)
	Debit
	Card Security Check
Post-Screen	Geolocation
	Fraud Scoring
	Modeling
	Reverse Address & Phone Lookups
	Credit Checks
Review	Call Back Consumer
	Call Bank
	Cross Check of Buying History
	Query Order Activity
Accounting	Settlements
	Credits
	Charge-back Processing
	Sharing & Updating Information with Peers and Partners
	Educations
	Tuning of Strategy

The purpose of breaking the business process into phases is to make you look at your business process in terms of goals. For each phase there is a definitive goal of what you want to achieve. By looking at the business process in this fashion, you can look at new fraud techniques and more quickly envision where they fit into your strategy.

The pre-screen phase is used to review an order's information to determine acceptance criteria. This phase is typically automated, and it conducts rules and checks to attempt to completely rule out orders you will not do business with regardless of any other checks. In the pre-screen phase you are trying to weed out orders, with the intent of saving time and money. Why process authorizations or other fraud-prevention checks on an order if you know you won't take the order regardless of the outcome? Examples of orders being cut out here are those that are international, when the company only does business in the USA, or the rejecting of an order because the order contains data on your internal hot list.

In the payment phase you are conducting the processes and checks required to accept an order. This includes getting an authorization, address verification information and card security check data.

The post-screen phase is where you perform your advanced reviews on orders that have passed the pre-screen and payment phases. This includes using business logic as well as advanced fraud-prevention techniques. Typically the first thing you want to check in this phase is the positive list to see if you can automatically pass all other tests.

The review phase includes all of the post-screening checks you do to attempt to catch fraud or to convert orders. This phase is a manual phase, and can be as simple as doing spot checks on orders to having review queues and manual sorting.

The accounting phase starts once an order has been fully accepted and lasts until 12 months after the sale. This includes processing credits, settlements, reauthorizations, charge-backs and tuning of the overall fraud-prevention strategy.

Typically the pre-screen, payment and post-screen phases are automated and occur in real-time. The review and accounting phases will make use of automation tools but are mainly manual processes.

Designing a Strategy Based on Risk Exposure

One approach to designing a strategy is looking at the level of risk your company is exposed to. The higher your risk, the more you will rely on fraud-prevention techniques and the more extensive the checks will have to be.

For some merchants the level of risk they are exposed to is so small that the standard address verification and card security schemes offered by the credit card associations will be more than enough. For example the education, utilities and government sectors can reach out and touch their consumers, de-frauding them is much more unlikely. Not that it doesn't happen — it's just not that high of a concern.

The following chart provides a break out of fraud-prevention techniques by the level of risk a merchant is exposed to. View the three levels of risk and determine which category you fall into. In looking at the characteristics, they are not meant to be all-inclusive — you may only meet one or two of the criteria listed. These characteristics are meant to form a guide to determine the level of risk you may be exposed to.

Level of Risk	Description
Low Risk	• Looking for lowest-cost solution
	• Low volume
	• High margin
	• Clothing, utilities, tuition, insurance
	• Fraud rate less than .25% or total loss of dollars less than $5,000
Medium Risk	• Medium to high volume
	• Low to medium margin
	• High fencibility: electronics, toys, games, music, personal services, books, clothing, travel, international business
	• Fraud rate greater than .75% or total losses exceeds $50,000 per year
High Risk	• Medium to high volume
	• Low to medium margin
	• Very high fencibility: electronic downloads, high-end electronics, financial vehicles, gift cards, adult, gaming, rechargeable cell phones, travel, international business, credit line or card issuance
	• Fraud rate greater than 1% or total fraud losses exceeds $100,000 per year

	Low Risk	Medium Risk	High Risk
Authorization	•	•	•
Address Verification Service	•	•	•
Card Security	•	•	•
Consumer Authentications	•	•	•
MOD 10 Check	•	•	•
Smart Cards			
Hot Lists	•	•	•
Warm Lists		•	•
Positive Lists		•	•
Velocity of Use		•	•
Velocity of Change		•	•
Geolocation			•
Age Verification			•
Credit Check			•
Out-of-Pocket Checks			•
Fraud Screening		•	•
Internal Rules	•	•	•
Reverse Lookups		•	•
Return E-mail			
Deposit Check			•
Delivery Address Verification			•
Denied Party check	•	•	•
Manual Review			•
Neural Nets			•
Rules Engine		•	•
SecureTokens			•
Biometrics			•
E-Commerce Insurance			•

Chapter 10

Address Verification Services (AVS)

Address Verification Services (AVS) is a tool provided by credit card associations and issuing banks to allow merchants to check the submitted billing address in order to see if it is on file with the issuing bank. The AVS check is usually done as part of a merchant's request for authorization on the credit card. When a merchant makes a request, the address is checked against the address on file at the issuing bank. AVS is supported in the United States, Canada and the UK. Visa, MasterCard, American Express and Discover Card all support AVS. For other card types check with your payment processor.

How Good Is It?

The reliability of AVS is suspect. There a lot of viable reasons why the billing address the consumer gives a merchant could be different from what the issuing bank has on file. Reasons range from recent moves or smaller issuing banks that use third-party services who can't keep the records up to date, to frequently traveling consumers who use a family member's address as the address of record. AVS is not a good indicator for fraudulent activity. The fact is if a merchant implements AVS incorrectly they could drop between 5% and 28% of their good orders.

Here are other key features of AVS:
- It will help in disputing charge-backs because you have a transaction in which the consumer's billing address on the order is the same as what is on file at the issuing bank.

- It only verifies the first five digits of the address and the zip code. Still possible to have returned goods if the consumer simply makes a typo when entering his or her address.
- This should be one of the first fraud-prevention capabilities a merchant should implement. If a merchant has not been using AVS today they should be. Implementing AVS is easy, and it can help them in prioritizing the orders they want to review.

Considerations When Implementing or Buying This Functionality

- AVS is only available from banks. Merchants that are using payment software or gateways that talk about AVS should understand that these applications and services only support the AVS information flow and cannot offer a merchant the actual AVS check.
- AVS in the UK is set up differently than the U.S. In the UK the AVS and card security check are combined in the same request and in the same response code, whereas in the U.S. the AVS and card security check are separated.
- If you are a merchant, you should contact your payment processor on the use and implementation of AVS. The AVS check is typically done as part of the authorization call and is done in real time on the e-commerce engine. In implementing AVS, you will have to have logic to interpret the codes that your payment processor sends back to you. You will need to properly route the order based on the information you get back from the payment processor.
- Typically it takes anywhere from a day to a week to implement AVS into your order process. The keys to quickly implementing AVS are to make sure you have a clear plan on what you want to do with an order, based on the return code from the AVS check.

Estimated Costs – Merchants can only get AVS from their credit card authorization request. There is no extra cost associated with getting this information, but merchants will need to make changes to their systems to handle the return codes.

Alternative Solutions – Merchants can look at delivery address verification, reverse lookups or geolocation validation.

Vendors – Any acquiring bank or third-party payment processor

Chapter 10

How Does it Work?

AVS, or Address Verification, is a tool provided by credit card associations and issuing banks to allow merchants to check the submitted billing address to see if it is on file with the issuing bank. The AVS check is usually done as part of the merchant's request for authorization on the card. When a merchant makes a request, the address is checked against the address on file at the issuing bank. Only the first four to five digits of the address and the zip code are verified – everything else IS NOT CHECKED.

Example:
> Mr. John Doe
> 1234 USA Street
> Realtown, ST 56789

What would be sent to the issuing bank to be checked would be "1234" and "56789"

Merchants will get one of six codes back from their payment processor indicating what matched: full match, partial match-address, partial match-zip code, no match, international and unavailable. Using AVS as part of their risk solution is very beneficial but relying solely on AVS is very dangerous. If a merchant implemented a rule in their solution that said they would only take orders that are a full match on AVS, they would have a very high insult rate, as the information contained in the issuing bank can be old, or the items being purchased could be as gifts. Merchants would leave a lot of business on the table if they implemented this type of rule.

Likewise getting a full match for AVS should tell a merchant something as well: that there is less risk. If the order's address information is on file with the issuing bank and the merchant is shipping to the record on file, the consumer would have a hard time disputing they did not make the charge.

Regardless of the AVS return value, merchants can still get a valid authorization on a card. If a merchant got a no match that would be termed a "soft decline" in the eyes of the banks.

How Do I Use the Results?

In the United States, AVS is the most common tool merchants reported using to help prevent fraud. According to the CyberSource Merchant Fraud Survey 2002, 71% of the merchants surveyed are using it. The UK is very early in its rollout of AVS, with Visa EU reporting only 6% merchant usage in early 2003.

In general, merchants should anticipate the majority of their orders coming in as a full match — plan on between 40 to 80%. Visa EU reported in early 2003 that they were seeing a 75% full match rate with those merchants that were using the new AVS service. Just because a merchant gets a response of partial match or no match does indicate increased risk in accepting an order. Remember AVS is not a good indicator of fraud. In case studies the highest actual fraud losses for any one AVS response code was only 11%, meaning 89% of the orders were valid and good orders. Some merchants will experience much higher fraud losses than this, but there are other rules, and fraud-prediction tools that will better isolate fraudulent behavior without sacrificing sales conversion.

Likewise getting a response from AVS of unavailable or international does not indicate increased risk either, with most merchants reporting the combined fraud losses for these two response codes being less than AVS full match. Some businesses can and will experience a much higher incidence of international fraud than others. This is especially true for digitally downloadable goods and services.

When evaluating how well AVS is doing for a merchant, don't get trapped by the percent of fraud for any one given AVS response value. If you remember earlier in this discussion we pointed out that the highest percentage of orders will be AVS full match so the highest concentration of dollars at risk will be there, and typically the smallest fraud percentage of loss will also be found on AVS full match. This gives merchants a false sense of security that AVS full match doesn't need their attention on fraud prevention, when this is the greatest number of dollars at risk, and the easiest way to fool most merchant's internal screening procedures.

There are cases in which merchants do have very specific and significant skews on fraud in international and in no match categories. If the skew occurs, this is typically a sign of a fraud attack on the location, site or store.

Building This In-House

A merchant can easily implement checks to try and verify the consumer's address, but a merchant cannot build anything that can give them the same check to the bank records. If a merchant really wants to try and verify this information further they can do any of the following

Manual Review - Call the issuing bank to verify the data
Manual Review - Perform a reverse lookup of the data

Chapter 11

Advanced Address Verification (AAV)

Advanced Address Verification (AAV) is used to validate the shipping address of American Express orders in which the shipping address is different from the billing address.

How Good Is It?

AAV+ is a real-time solution for merchants doing e-commerce, mail order or phone orders. AAV+ is not the same as AVS. AVS is checking the billing address on file with the Issuing Bank, AAV+ is checking the shipping address. The service is provided exclusively by American Express and is intended to check the billing and shipping address when the two addresses are different. This service does offer an optional guarantee.
  AAV:
- Allows a merchant to take orders that may have been deemed too risky before.
- Reduces the costs for manual reviews in which the transaction is from American Express and a merchant has done the AAV+ check.
- Covers a merchant's charge-backs on American Express transactions run through the service.

Considerations When Implementing or Buying This Functionality

Limitations of AAV include:
- It only works for American Express transactions.

- If a merchant doesn't have a direct connection to American Express, they need to make sure their payment processor can handle the new data fields required for this service.
- It does not guarantee customer service charge-backs, only fraudulent charge-backs.

Estimated Costs – There are different fees for using the service and getting the charge-back guarantee.

Alternative Solutions – Many vendors provide address verification services ranging from delivery address verification to full verification based on credit bureau and government record checks.

Vendors – American Express.

How Does it Work?

To use the service a merchant needs to make sure their payment processor supports the new service. If a merchant has a direct connection to American Express they can immediately start looking at how to implement this solution.

Once a merchant has decided to implement the AAV+ solution they will have to notify American Express to get a copy of the AAV+ specifications. American Express will conduct a walkthrough of the specifications if they desire it.

With the specifications a merchant can begin to modify their authorization format. Once a merchant has made the modifications, American Express will have to certify their format and review their ordering system script, and/or checkout page, for their website. Then a merchant can begin to send orders.

With AAV+ a merchant will be sending the following new data in their authorization feed:

Card member Billing Information:
Card member Billing Address, Zip code and Phone Number
Card member Name as it appears on the card

Alternate Address Information:
Ship to Street Address, Zip Code and Phone Number
Ship to First and Last Name

Ship to Country Code (ISO Numeric)

How Do I Use the Results?

A merchant will get a response from American Express indicating if the data was a match. If it is and a merchant has purchased the guarantee, they can immediately accept the order. If they don't have the guarantee then they have to decide on the order. If it is a match on the name, phone and address, the merchant's risk is greatly reduced.

Building This In-House

A merchant can purchase data volumes that give them yellow page-type information that they can do checks against.

Chapter 12

Age Verification

Age verification is the attempt to determine the age of the consumer at the time of purchase. Typically it is used for regulatory compliance in the adult, alcohol, and gaming sectors.

How Good Is It?

The reliability of age verification is directly related to the country that the consumer resides in. Most of the vendors that supply this service rely on public records to determine age. Some vendors rely on credit reports.

Completing an age verification check for consumers:

- Can help a merchant ensure that they don't lose their liquor license for selling to underage consumers.
- Can ensure a merchant of an adult site doesn't get hit with heavy fines.
- Can ensure a gaming merchant doesn't get in trouble with national laws governing the age of consumers playing games of chance or placing bets.

Considerations When Implementing or Buying This Functionality

- If a merchant is using a vendor that uses credit reports, they may be required to ask their consumer for social security numbers or for their National Insurance Number if they reside in the United Kingdom.
- Does the service provider offer guarantees or reimbursement for fines or legal fees associated with the use of the service?

- Set up a system of "accounts" so age verification is run only once per consumer, not for every purchase they make.

Estimated Costs – Typically this service is offered on a per-transaction basis. Some vendors offer a subscription-based model for payment.

Alternative Solutions – Drivers license fax back, use of a "over 18" or "over 21" web page, in which the consumer has to click on a checkbox that states that they are over this age in order to continue on the website.

Vendors – Aristotle's VerifyMe, Paymentech OnGuard & Verisign (uses Aristotle's VerifyMe – www.verifymyidentification.com), Experian. For card-present operations check out VerifyIDs.com, AVS.co.uk (Adult only), AdultSights.

How Does it Work?

The typical age verification service requires that a merchant provide the consumer's name, address and phone number. Some services will require that a merchant also provide the social security number.

Depending on the service a merchant uses, they will either get an actual age or date of birth back. Merchants will still have to do some logic to ensure the age is acceptable, or the service will provide a set of answers such as:

Over 21
Over 18
Under 18
Unable to verify
Unavailable

Some service providers will provide financial guarantees for legal fees and fines if the government comes after a merchant and they used the service. Remember a merchant only has to check a consumer once, so make sure to add logic that checks to see if a new consumer has already been checked before.

How Do I Use the Results?

If the age verification service provides a hard age then:

1. Determine which field holds the age, or date of birth field
2. If date of birth was given, create a formula to determine the age
3. Create a rule to compare the provided age with their age requirements

If their age verification service provides a descriptive result then check to see which result was returned and make sure it meets the regulatory requirements, for instance, over 18 or over 21.

Building This In-House

Use a process of account set up in which you ask the consumer to provide a copy of their government-issued ID to keep on file. They fax it in to the merchant. A merchant only has to do this once for a consumer, and then they can buy anytime they want.

Set up a webpage that asks the consumer to certify they are over 18 or 21 by clicking on a certification button on the page that won't let them continue if they don't certify. Make sure you keep a record of this "acceptance" on file.

Chapter 13

Authorization (Real Time)

Authorization is a request from the merchant to the consumer's issuing bank to determine if sufficient money is available on the credit card for payment, and to hold those funds for this purchase.

How Good Is It?

There are two methods merchants use to do authorizations: online (which is real time) or batch. If a merchant cannot successfully authorize a purchase on a credit card they will not be able to convert it. Doing real-time authorizations allows a merchant to quickly weed out consumers that don't have the money to make a purchase. It also gives a merchant the means to let the consumer know, while the consumer is still on the merchant's site, that they don't have funds so they can try another card.

Things to know about authorizations include:

- Authorizations do expire so a merchant needs to make sure they are still good when they want to settle their transaction
- A real-time authorization check allows a merchant to find out if funds are available. As a positive indicator the fact a consumer has funds available is positive point in converting a sale, but this is not a good indicator for fraudulent behavior.

Considerations When Implementing or Buying This Functionality

- Exceeding a consumer's card limits: In some cases merchants can exceed a consumer's credit card limit by mistake because they are running an authorization, and the consumer may fail one of the other checks the merchant requires for processing, and instead of using the original authorization they run another authorization. This can deplete the consumer's credit line even though the other orders are not going to be processed.

- Some merchants try to cancel an authorization, but this is not really supported by all issuing banks, and usually requires a phone call to the bank. Even with that there is no guarantee that the bank will reverse the authorization.
- What types of reports do they offer to reconcile transactions on a daily, monthly and annual basis?
- Do they charge separately for authorizations and settlements
- Can settlements be done in real time or batch?
- Do they support AVS, card security schemes and e-commerce indicator field?
- Can they process all of the major card types, or do they have to have a separate feed for American Express or Discover? Or if they want separate feeds to keep the costs down, can the application or service support that?

Estimated Costs – Costs associated with getting an authorization vary widely. There are service bureaus that offer a transactional fee for each call. This is usually very inexpensive – a couple of pennies to less than fifteen cents per transaction. The more volume a merchant does, typically the smaller their transactional fees. For small businesses, most major vendors offer special discounted prices for them, but they are limited to the number of transactions they can run. Vendors also provide payment software solutions that will allow merchants to connect to bank or payment processors to conduct their acquiring activities. Merchants will typically pay a moderate up-front cost for the software then an annual maintenance fee for the software. If they will be using a frame connection to access real-time payment, they will need at least 30 days for the certification process, and the cost of the line should be taken into consideration, as they are significantly more expensive than other options.

Alternative Solutions – If a merchant is a small business I would recommend they look at aggregators for their business. These are businesses that service multiple merchants, called multi-merchants, and they can provide payment solutions at lower costs for smaller merchants by pooling a bunch of merchants together to keep costs down.

Vendors – CyberSource, Clear Commerce, Paymentech, Wells Fargo, Chase, FDMS, Verisign, Retail Decisions, Retail Logic,

How Does it Work?

The issuing bank only checks the consumer's credit card number for authorization. They confirm if it is an active account, if sufficient funds are available, and check AVS (Address Verification System).

There are generally two types of declines a merchant can receive with an authorization: soft or hard declines. Soft declines are those declines in which the bank requires further verification. The bank has not given authorization at this time.

The reasons the bank may want to be contacted are:

- Additional security is in place with banks regarding Internet companies.
- A bank wants to talk with the Credit Department and then contact the customer to verify the purchase is valid.
- Some banks may have a list of Internet companies they will allow authorizations to go through.
- A customer may have a limit for authorization on their card and the bank needs to contact them to verify the purchase before authorization can be given to avoid possible fraud.

Soft declines have a high percentage rate of converting.

A hard decline from the bank is when the return from the authorization is:

- Insufficient available credit
- Possible fraud – lost or stolen card
- Invalid credit card – number does not exist
- System error
- Time out

System error orders should be actively worked on to try to convert them.

How Do I Use the Results?

Real-time versus batch processing – in general it is our recommendation that a merchant implement and use a real-time authorization service. Doing real-time authorizations will help a merchant cut their overall costs by cutting out those transactions that they would not be able to be converted regardless of fraud because the consumer doesn't have any money. If a merchant is doing batch authorizations, they now have to store the transaction, run it against the system if it fails, and contact the consumer for another credit card. Had the merchant been doing real-time authorizations the consumer could have provided another credit card when they were at the site or when they were on the phone. A merchant will also have a higher number of call center calls as these transactions usually will lead to customer service calls in which the consumer calls to find our why his or her orders aren't there yet.

Building This In-House

All banks and processors publish specifications that allow merchants to build their own solutions to communicate payment processing. A merchant will have to get their solution certified with the banking institution. With the number of payment solutions on the marketplace, and the reduction in prices to purchase these solutions over the last couple of years, I would recommend that a merchant not build in-house for the following reasons:

- It is cheaper to purchase these solutions on the open market than build them.
- The payment processing and credit card specifications change constantly, sometimes several times in a year, and a merchant doesn't want to have to keep recoding their solution and getting it recertified.
- Commercial solutions have already been certified by the banking institutions and usually offer multiple links to different banking institutions, allowing a merchant to easily switch between banks for better rates.
- The security found in the commercial solutions is typically more robust than in-house solutions and this provides greater protection from unauthorized access attempts.

Chapter 14

Biometrics

Biometrics are used to verify a person's identity by a unique physical attribute that distinguishes that individual from any other person. Common physical elements used are (but not limited to) fingerprints, retinal scans, voiceprints and DNA match.

How Good Is It?

The use of biometrics is very effective as a tool to authenticate a person's identity. The problem is that it is very expensive to implement and requires the consumer to have equipment to produce the authentication. For today's marketplace it is very unlikely that this type of fraud technique will be implemented in any kind of mass scale. If you have a defined set of consumers who constantly make purchases you may entertain this option. But more than likely you are in a very high-risk regulated sector if you are entertaining this fraud-prevention technique. For example, the pharmaceutical sector would be well suited.

- Merchants may still have "application fraud" in which the account is set up in the fraudster's identity with their biometric readings.
- Very expensive to implement, very small-scale type of solution.
- Requires the consumer to have specialized equipment to perform the authentication check.
- Most solutions still store authentication data on hard drives that could be hacked.
- A lot of devices give the option of defaulting to a password instead of a biometric authentication.

Considerations When Implementing or Buying This Functionality

- Are the merchant's consumers setting up accounts? How will the merchant collect the initial biometric data from their consumer.
- What type of equipment will the consumer need to perform the check?
- Are the devices portable, or will they only work on the one system they are installed on?
- How do they work for MOTO?
- What happens if the system cannot authenticate, and it is the real consumer?
- What are the insult rates of the solution?
- Who supports the consumer in getting the technology to work?
- Hardware compatibility issues.

Estimated Costs – Very Expensive

Alternative Solutions – RSA tokens, authentication schemes with passwords or codes

Vendors – Identix, BioLink, Ethentica, Touchcredit

How Does it Work?

These devices compare a stored image or value that is calculated by the unique characteristics of the consumer with the value they use when they make a purchase. For example, with fingerprints they may be counting the number of identical points from a pre-saved image of the consumer's thumb.

How Do I Use the Results?

These tools can be implemented in a number of different ways. The merchant could send their consumer the device and have him or her install it upon registering with the merchant's solution provider. Then when the consumer attempts to make a purchase, the system would do a validation and pass the information on to the merchant.

Another method is to have the device perform the authentication and produce a one-use number for the purchase, like a disposable credit card number. In some cases the device actually performs the authentication as a means for gaining access to the site or material for making a purchase.

Building This In-House

N/A

Chapter 15

Card Security Schemes

The CV number is a tool for merchants to verify that the consumer is in possession of the card. This helps to prevent fraud in which the fraudster may have acquired the credit card number in the trash or online, but is not in possession of the physical card so they cannot give this extra set of numbers. This number is a three or four digit number located either above the credit card number for American Express cards or on the back for MasterCard and Visa.

These numbers have been in place for a while, and have been slowly adopted by merchants. You are more likely now to be asked for this number when you are trying to complete a MOTO transaction than a year and half ago. The Discover card was one of the last cards to implement this technology. At this time all of the issuing and acquiring banks should support this technology, but a few smaller holdouts may still exist.

How Good Is It?

Implementing card security checks, such as CV, CVV2 etc., has shown the ability to reduce the number of fraudulent attempts. It has also shown that it will cause a nominal reduction in sales conversion for online transactions. Merchants do not have to actually check the card security number to get the reduction in fraud attempts. Merchants should expect an increase in call center calls when they implement card security for the first time. The use of card security schemes by merchants is on the rise but the vast majority of merchants still do not use card security. MOTO has had a higher take-up on card security schemes than e-commerce.

- In the UK, card security schemes are not even recommended for use by e-commerce merchants by Visa EU.
- The intent of card verification is to attempt to verify that the consumer using the card is in possession of the card.
- Good for catching fraudsters attempting to use stolen credit card information from online or through other means like the trash, or through other card activity.
- Good at catching fraudsters who gained access to cards via skimming.

Adoption of card verification has increased dramatically in the last 12 months, call center-based operations have picked up the use more heavily than e-commerce.

Considerations When Implementing or Buying This Functionality

- When a merchant implements this check on their website they will have to change their credit card submittal screen to show a picture of the credit card and where to find this number because a lot of consumers have no idea what this number is. It can cause some confusion and some additional customer service calls to complete an order.
- Does not actually verify that the cardholder is making the purchase.
- Not all consumers understand what this number is on their card.
- Make sure all payment processors or banking institutions in use for payment support the card security check data elements.

Estimated Costs – There are no extra costs to run the Card Security Check

Alternative Solutions – None

Vendors – Any banking institution

How Does it Work?

The card security code is a three- or four-digit value. It has been implemented as a security feature to help stop counterfeit cards, and use of card numbers without the physical card. The value provides a cryptographic check of the information embossed on the card.

The three-digit number is derived from the card account number by means of an algorithm and a "seed." It is possible to have repeat numbers — about every 900 cards there is a repeat. There would never be a number of all zeros or all zeros and a single one.

The card security value is printed on the signature panel on the back of Visa cards immediately following the Visa card account number or on the front of American Express and Discover cards just after the account number.

CVV2

The Card Security Scheme validates two things:

- The customer has a card in his/her possession.
- The card account is legitimate.

The card security number is not contained in the magnetic stripe information, nor does it appear on sales receipts. Using the card security scheme helps to prevent merchants from receiving counterfeit cards or being a victim of fraud.

For transactions conducted over the Internet, you may ask cardholders for their CVV2 online. Their Internet screen might include these elements, for example:

```
┌─────────────────────────────────────────────────────────┐
│  Visa Account Number: ┌──────────────────────────┐       │
│                       └──────────────────────────┘       │
│                                                           │
│  Card Expiration Date: ┌──────────────┐                  │
│                        │   MM/YY       │                  │
│                        └──────────────┘                  │
│                                                           │
│  3-Digit Value: ┌──────┐      ○    Click here if your card│
│                 │ XXX  │            has no three-digit number.│
│                 └──────┘                                  │
│                                                           │
│  Please enter the 3-digit value at the end of your account│
│  number printed on the back of your Visa card.            │
└─────────────────────────────────────────────────────────┘
```

Include CVV2 in Authorization Requests
Authorization requests must include at least:

- Account number
- Expiration date
- CVV2 value
- Transaction dollar amount

To learn more about the benefits of CVV2 and CVV2 technical requirements, contact the card association.

How Do I Use the Results?

When a merchant processed their authorization call they will get back a "match" or "no match" response. If they receive a no-match I recommend an auto decline. Merchants should tell the consumer they cannot validate the card security number they submitted, and ask them to call in their order to their call center. This allows the merchant to coach a legitimate consumer to find the card security number.

Building This In-House

Implementing this service as part of the back-end process is not a major initiative, and requires mostly data element changes. Updates need to be made to the front end to allow consumers to input the new data points. Merchants will have to provide some visual aids for the consumer.

Chapter 16

Charge Verification

Used by merchants to validate card member information from the issuing bank or card association by physically contacting them and asking them to validate the cardholder information.

How Good Is It?

The charge verification services available today do not offer any kind of guarantee for fraudulent transactions. They provide extra security for accepting orders, allowing you to confirm more of the consumer's data. There is significant difference between the card types and the ability to call and confirm consumer's data. This ranges from the Visa and MasterCard Code 10 procedures or American Expresses Charge Verification Program to manually contacting the issuing bank of the consumer's credit card for validation. Merchants are really just trying to confirm if the cardholder information they have is the same data the bank has on file. If a merchant can confirm the billing data with the issuing bank they should still confirm the order with the consumer to create the complete loop.

Charge verification:

- Offers no guarantee on charge-backs
- Cannot be automated
- Has different rules and levels of service for each card type and bank
- Will not always contact the card member on file to validate the order — only American Express's program offers this at this time

Considerations When Implementing or Buying This Functionality

- Time-intensive process — adds at least 24 hours to the processing time to accept the order
- Who will place the calls?
- How will responses from the banks or institutions be handled?
- How will orders be selected for this process?

Estimated Costs – The merchant will have to have manpower ready to handle the calls. Costs will be directly in response to the number of orders taken and the number of orders that will require call backs.

Alternative Solutions – Use an automated process such as fraud screening, Advanced Address Verification Plus by American Express, or third-party consumer authentication services. Reverse lookups.

Vendors – American Express, Visa, MasterCard, Discover Card.

Typical Usage Method – Manual Review

How Does it Work?

Technically a merchant is only supposed to call these numbers if they suspect fraud, but that is a very "qualitative" standard. So as a general rule, if a merchant wasn't going to take the order due to the checks they already did, then they should perform this check so they can at least try to convert the order.

Each Credit Card type is a little different on their rules for charge verification, so check with an acquiring bank on what processes they recommend for each.

American Express offers a Charge Verification Group that will attempt to verify the purchase for a merchant.

- Must be a card-not-present transaction
- Physical goods only, with value greater than $200

American Express will contact the card member to confirm the sale. The American Express representative will reply to the merchant with a yes or no response. (Note if American Express cannot reach the card member the merchant will not get a response)

How Do I Use the Results?

Based on the response a merchant gets, they will have to decide if they want to accept the order. Remember they cannot validate shipping information, only the billing information. If they used American Express and they got a confirmation from the card member, they should accept the order. If they were able to confirm the billing information with the bank, then call the card member directly and validate the purchase with them. Don't call the card member first, they may have given bogus information in the order. When calling a consumer where you suspect fraud, always confirm the phone number with the issuing bank and use only that number to contact the consumer.

Building This In-House

Set up a person or team of people to conduct the charge verification process. Be sure to document the process and steps the team members should follow in doing the charge verification. Documenting the process and steps for verification is important, even in a one-person shop, to make sure nothing is overlooked. As a general rule, fraud review personnel can always do more than what is written down, but never less.

Chapter 17

Consumer Authentication

"Consumer authentication" is a blanket term to discuss emerging tools that are intended to validate that the authorized credit card holder is the one actually attempting to make a purchase. Visa calls their consumer authentication service "Verified by Visa," and MasterCard calls their service "MasterCard SecureCode." American Express does not offer any similar service today, but has indicated that they are looking into the program.

How Good Is It?

In general the concept of authenticating the consumer is a good one. For the merchant, this is an excellent tool since it is one of the first tools that actually offers some financial coverage if fraud does occur. The card associations implemented these programs to increase consumer confidence in making purchases online, and to help protect online merchants from fraud.

The main reason a merchant wants to implement this service is the protection it offers from fraud-related charge-backs. Not everything is protected, so be sure to review the details of the program with Visa and MasterCard. There are significant differences on what is covered in the United States versus what is covered in Europe. Some examples of what is not covered by the program include: Purchases made with procurement cards, recurring billing, split shipments or back-ordered goods and "one-click" technology sales and transactions in which the consumer cannot be authenticated.

It also seems that certain high-risk segments, such as adult and gaming, are not going to be covered, so merchants in these vertical markets should check with Visa or MasterCard before they implement this technique. There is no threshold set for risk, but there is wording that suggests a threshold for fraud rates will be set and merchants will have to keep their losses below that. Also merchants have to properly set the e-commerce-preferred indicator.

The other major benefit of the consumer authentication tools is the simplification of some of their charge-back resolution activities. For those orders in which the consumer was participating in the program and they did authenticate them, the resolution process would occur between the issuing bank and the consumer, not between the merchant and the consumer.

Consumers may be legitimate even if they can't authenticate. Some examples of reasons why good customers may not be able to authenticate include:

- The use of software that prevents pop-up windows will render this service obsolete, the pop-up can time out
- Consumers that were pre-registered may not know that they have a password or PIN to authenticate properly

Considerations When Implementing or Buying This Functionality

- The current consumer authentication tools offered by Visa and MasterCard are meant for, and work only on, e-commerce transactions. Merchants still need to have fraud processes in place to handle MOTO traffic.
- For these programs to work the merchant, consumer, issuer and acquiring bank must all be participating in the program. So make sure to verify that the acquiring bank supports these programs prior to set up. Merchants will also need to verify the acquiring bank certification requirements.
- For European merchants, some of the acquiring banks are still not set up to support consumer authentication.
- Merchants still need to perform other fraud checks — this tool does not cover many of the card types on the market today. Likewise there are legitimate cases in which a merchant may not be able to complete the authentication process with the consumer. Merchants still need to make sure their overall fraud rates are kept within acceptable levels and industry experts expect to see some fraud shifts to cards not offering this service.

- For companies doing little transactional volume, they should consider using an outsourced service bureau to perform this service.
- Always check and provide all of the correct data points: Merchants have to make sure they are supplying all of the correct data elements or they may not get the guarantee offered in the program. Confirm that the e-commerce indicator, ECI, is used, and AVS was checked. Likewise the CAVV/AVV needs to show the order was checked for enrollment. Additionally the XID (the unique transaction number) must be with the order.
- Merchants will have to get a digital certificate, which takes some time to get. Merchants have to get it from Visa or MasterCard. Expect two weeks for this process. The acquiring bank can provide the forms for merchants to start the process.

Estimated Costs – Merchants can find this service available as an outsourced service, or as a software application that can be implemented in-house. The actual cost to purchase the software is fairly low (it costs a couple of thousand dollars to purchase). Merchants will have to pay annual maintenance on the software and will have to make changes to their front-end e-commerce engines.

Alternative Solutions – Commercially available consumer authentication.

Vendors – Arcot, Cardinal Commerce, CyberSource, Clear Commerce.

How Does it Work?

The process used by the consumer authentication services to authenticate consumers is pretty simple. The consumer enrolls with the issuing bank and is given a password, PIN or device to authenticate themselves. When the consumer makes a purchase online the consumer is asked to give that password, PIN or device to authenticate.

The purchase sequence can be broken down into five stages, first the consumer goes through the check-out procedure, the same way they do today, providing the same data fields they do today. When the buy button is pressed on their system, using the commercially available software on the market, it sends a message to the card association (i.e., Visa or MasterCard), to find out if the consumer is participating in the consumer authentication program. If the consumer is participating in the program, the card association service will send a pop-up window to the consumer. The pop-up looks like it is coming from the consumer's issuing bank. The pop-up asks the consumer to enter their password or PIN. The issuing bank then validates this password or PIN and returns the results to the merchant.

For these programs to work the merchant, consumer, issuer and acquiring bank must all be participating in the program. Consumer adoption is slow at best. According to Visa, about 10 million cardholders are enrolled as of October 2002. Likewise merchant adoption has been slow too. Merchant enrollment should increase in the United States as of April 2003, when the financial coverage for certain orders took affect.

Consumers are being enrolled by self-registration, issuer auto enrollment, and issuer prompted registration.

The liability shift is different based on the region you are doing business in, the type of charge-back you have and the type of card. For the Visa program you will be covered from charge-backs that are coded as RC23, RC61 and RC75. For MasterCard only charge-backs coded as RC37 are covered right now. For the Visa program you only have to check to see if they are enrolled to get coverage. Remember if they are enrolled and they can't authenticate you get no liability shift. Currently for European transaction, in which the cardholder and merchant are European, you have the liability shift for both card types. For the United States the liability shift for Visa started in April 2003 and for MasterCard a date had not been announced as of the writing of this book.

From a security perspective, all communication between the consumer and issuing bank is secured. A merchant will not see or ask for this password. The pop-up window the end user receives contains a secret message that only the consumer knows, that shows the consumer that the pop-up window is real and not a fake. This is to reassure the consumer base that someone is not trying to steal the password from them.

There has been a fraud case in which fraudsters acquired account information and then called the issuing bank and changed the address information and signed up for the Verified by Visa program. The fraudsters then made fraudulent orders on these accounts. The merchants will be covered as long as they followed the rules.

These programs are excellent deterrents, but they are not "silver bullets" that will end all fraud. In reality the majority of merchants that are implementing the Verified by Visa and MasterCard SecureCode programs today are doing so not to combat fraud but to attract new consumers that were not comfortable with using the Internet for making purchases before these services were available. In the article "Visa Starts Password Service to Fight Online Fraud," By Saul Hansell, The New York Times on the Web,

Published on December 3, 2001, Hansell quotes Dell Computers as one of the merchants looking to the Verified by Visa program to help give customers more confidence buying online.

How Do I Use the Results?

For Visa and MasterCard orders when merchants are using this technology they should implement the following:

- For orders in which the consumer is participating in the program, the order type is a covered type, and the consumer successfully authenticates, accept the order.
- For orders in which the consumer is not participating in the program, the order type is a covered type, the merchant has checked for enrollment, and the order characteristics are within their normal order tolerances, accept the order.
- For orders in which the consumer is not participating in the program, the order type is a covered type, the merchant has checked for enrollment, and the order characteristics are not in-line with their normal orders, review the order or perform further fraud checks favoring sales conversion.
- For orders in which the consumer is participating in the program, and cannot successfully authenticate and the order characteristics are in line with their normal orders; perform other fraud-screening checks or manually review the order favoring risk aversion.
- For non-Visa and MasterCard orders perform traditional checks.

Chapter 18

Credit Check

The credit check technique is used to check a consumer's identity by comparing information the consumer provided to what is stored on their credit report.

How Good Is It?

This is an effective way to verify data a consumer is providing a merchant. In general the credit report can validate the phone number, address, name and credit card information provided. Merchants can also use it to verify age.

- Can be manipulated by a fraudster in cases of true identity theft
- Can be expensive to use for authentication
- These reports rely on input from agencies, banks and merchants and their data may not be completely up to date
- Typically requires the social security number (SSN), or the last four digits of it, to be provided
- Depending on the data a merchant accesses they may have further legal notification requirements in accordance with the Fair Credit Reporting Act

Considerations When Implementing or Buying This Functionality

- Most consumers are not going to want to give a merchant their SSN and credit card number.
- Can you get data without a SSN?
- Can it support data on international orders?

- What data elements do they require from a merchant?
- Can they tell you about recent changes to the data?
- Don't ever store credit card and SSN information together unless proper security precautions have been put in place. If a merchant gets hacked and this information is compromised, it is going to hurt.

Estimated Costs - Moderate, typically a per-transaction fee

Alternative Solutions - Reverse lookups: phone and address, consumer authentication

Vendors - Equifax, Experian, TransUnion

How Does it Work?

As merchants are processing an order they will collect the required data elements from the consumer and will pass them to the credit bureau. Typically this information is sent through a real-time feed that hooks into their existing order processing or CRM application.

Typically the credit bureaus will have different levels of service as to what type of information they will return back to a merchant. They could have verification-only checks, fraud score checks and true credit scores. Make sure the information provided by the service will meet the requirements for using them.

Accessing a consumer's credit history is a big deal, so make sure to get legal guidance about what information is being accessed and if there is any new reporting or notification requirements that will have to be put into place.

How Do I Use the Results?

The feed a merchant gets back from the credit bureau may come in one of two forms. The first one is where they simply provide the information on the consumer. For example the merchant provided a name and a SSN and the credit bureau provided the merchant with an address, phone number and credit card number.

Or a merchant will provide them with the name, SSN, address, phone and credit card and they pass back a pass/fail indicator for each data element. Depending on how their choice of credit bureau works, the merchant will have to code their systems to interpret these results. The merchant will have to determine the criteria for accepting or rejecting an order.

Building This In-House

N/A

Chapter 19

Deposit Check

Deposit check is used to validate the consumer by depositing an amount of money into their bank account and having them validate the amount of money that was deposited.

How Good Is It?

The deposit check was primarily used by PayPal for validating customers. As a general rule this is a good method to validate a person's identity, but it does have limitations. As we all know true identity theft is a real issue, and in these cases fraudsters can set up bank accounts that look completely legitimate. Over 700,000 cases of identity theft were reported last year.

This check is not really good for traditional retail or businesses that are looking to have a one-time real-time purchase process. This is better suited to businesses that are establishing long-term arrangements with consumers in which the consumer will be coming back over and over for services, such as subscription services.

- Doesn't catch true identity theft cases
- Costly to set up, merchants have to put money on the line for setting up accounts
- Timely, merchants introduce a longer time period to close an order because the consumer has to go back and validate the deposit. This can take up to month to validate a consumer.

Considerations When Implementing or Buying This Functionality

- Will the solution need to support credit cards and bank accounts?

- Does the solution need to be able to credit back the initial purchase amount in future sales?
- Some consumers want instant gratification; make sure the solution will meet the needs of the consumer base that the merchant services. Also make sure the consumer base feels enough loyalty and desire to use the service that they will still be around to complete this process.
- From a consumer perspective this is a very long and burdensome process.

Estimated Costs – High

Alternative Solutions – Consumer authentication, out-of-wallet checks

Vendors – None

How Does it Work?

It's a three-step process:

When a new consumer comes to do business, a merchant will need to set up a new account for them. The merchant will get their credit card information or bank account information, address and phone number. They will notify the consumer that they will be making a deposit, if banking, and a charge if credit cards. The charge, and/or deposit, will be between $0.01 and $5.00. The merchant tells the consumer that they will receive an e-mail when the deposit or charge has been made, and they will have to validate the deposit or charge by responding to the e-mail.

Consumers can get this information by accessing their bank or credit card information online, by phone or when their statements come in. The merchant will receive an e-mail from the consumer with the amount they received or were charged. The merchant then validates this amount against their records. If they match they set up the account and proceed on. If not, they either decline the business or do a second deposit check.

How Do I Use the Results?

Whether a consumer passes or fails this test it is valuable information. Make sure you set up processes to maintain all credit card, bank account and demographic data to check future account set up attempts against them. This really helps with pre-screening transactions.

Building This In-House

Remember that a merchant needs to have good systems in place to check for consumers that are failing multiple times. Also make sure to implement positive lists, hot lists and warm lists to prevent fraudsters from working the site to get in.

Make sure to re-run the process on any new credit cards or bank accounts that are added to the account. Fraudsters will set up with a valid card, and then use bad cards inside the account.

Consider allowing consumers to place orders, or use the service, while they are being validated. Just don't allow fulfillment to take place, or for other valid orders to be superseded by these orders.

Put in velocity of use checks to see how many accounts are associated with a consumer's data points such as, address, phone number, credit card number and bank account number.

Chapter 20

Delivery Address Verification

Delivery address verification is used to check the consumer's shipping address to make sure it is a deliverable address.

How Good Is It?

The systems used to check addresses are typically the same ones the United States Postal Service uses to deliver mail. So they are good. Remember this service does not check to see if the consumer actually lives at that address, it just verifies that the address exists. The main use for this check is to ensure you don't have goods returned because the address is not deliverable. But this is also a good way to see if the consumer is using a real address or not.

- Doesn't validate that the consumer lives at the address, just that the address exists
- Much higher value for digitally delivered goods to make sure the consumer is not giving the merchant a bogus address
- Good for fulfillment, and for issues with lots of returned shipments due to undeliverable addresses
- Some of these services will auto-correct addresses to make sure they work correctly

Considerations When Implementing or Buying This Functionality

- Does the service provider support all of the countries required for the merchant's business?
- Address data changes constantly —how often is the data updated?

- Does the service know all of the actual numbers for post offices boxes or private mail-boxes? Does it capture suites?
- Does the service do address clean up?
- Does their provider give the merchant the following:
    o Validates the Incoming Address
    o Address Standardization
    o ZIP Correction and ZIP+4 Code Appending
    o Provides Line of Travel (LOT) Coding
    o Delivery Point Bar Coding
    o Distinguishes Residential and Business Addresses
    o Provides Carrier Route Codes and Carrier
    o Advanced Name and Address Parsing

Estimated Costs – For service bureaus you will pay for each transaction. For software services you will pay quarterly or monthly subscription fees for updates.

Alternative Solutions – Get address verification from credit bureaus or consumer authentication services.

Vendors – CyberSource, Group One Software, Untied States Postal Service, Intelligent Search Technology (CorrectAddress.com)

How Does it Work?

The service takes the shipping address information provided and checks to see if the address exists. It checks the street, city, state, zip code and country. Make sure to do the test in real time for the best results. Doing it in real time allows the merchant to immediately ask the consumer to correct the shipping data. For digital goods providers, use the billing address.

Some delivery address verification services will actually attempt to auto correct the address. It will put the zip into five-plus-four, and it will check the numbers and letters on addresses that have multiple units.

How Do I Use the Results?

If the delivery address verification check fails, make sure to ask the consumer to reconfirm the shipping address.

Building This In-House

1. Purchase software with address data
2. Create a call to the data to check the address

Or if a merchant wants to check this manually they can go to the USPS site to check the address as well.

Chapter 21

Denied Party Check

Denied party check is used to check the federal listing of parties that merchants in the U.S. are prohibited from doing business with. The intent is to automatically cross check in real-time consumer information against lists provided by the U.S. government of designated parties for whom it is illegal to ship, trade or sell goods and services.

U.S. regulations prohibit the sale (trade) of goods and/or services to certain entities and individuals, such as known terrorists and other restricted parties, contained in lists issued by various U.S. government agencies. The Office of Foreign Assets Control (OFAC) in the Department of Treasury publishes a denied party list of restricted entities and individuals.

How Good Is It?

There are providers of automated services and software to check for denied parties, and merchants can do this on their own. In general these solutions are fair, so make sure the solution that is chosen is using fuzzy logic. Fuzzy logic is the ability to see if the consumer data is similar to an entry on the denied party list. This is good to catch things such as abbreviations, misspelled words or variations.

Using a service means you don't have to maintain the list of denied parties, instead you are paying for each use of the service.

Features of denied party check include:

- It provides a way to screen orders with the posted listing without having to do significant coding
- It provides an automated way to update the information in the listing

- It provides a means for doing fuzzy logic matches
- It is not extendable to be industry specific
- It is available in the United States, Europe and Asia

Considerations When Implementing or Buying This Functionality

- What lists does the service get information from? For example, U.S. Government Anti-Terrorist, Embargoed Countries, International Traffic in Arms Debarment and Sanctions lists, and Specially Designated Nationals (SDN) and other Denied Persons lists, which may include terrorists, narcotics traffickers, and blocked persons and organizations.
- How often are the lists updated?
- Medical, drug and some high technology requirements differ greatly and merchants will have to put in significant updates to be compliant with these requirements for ensuring that they are not violating any laws.
- Does the service employ fuzzy logic for making matches?
- Is the service stand alone or part of a broader export compliance solution?

Estimated Costs – For service bureaus merchants will pay for each transaction, for software services they will pay quarterly or monthly subscription fees for updates.

Alternative Solutions – Some payment gateway services provide this service for free as part of their authorization services.

Vendors – CyberSource, Quova

How Does it Work?

Typically this check is done before the authorization or fraud screen is executed. There are several lists that are maintained by the U.S. government of persons or companies in the U.S., and abroad, with which U.S. businesses are not allowed to conduct trade. Lists include:

1. Specially Designated Nationals (SDN) list, including terrorists, narcotics traffickers, blocked persons and vessels. Issued by the Department of Treasury, Office of Foreign Assets Control.

2. Denied Persons List (BXA) U.S. Department of Commerce, issued by the Bureau of Export Administration, includes individuals that have violated export laws, shipping prohibited goods to.
3. Entity List, U.S. Issued by the Department of Commerce, The Bureau of Export Administration, includes foreign end users involved in proliferation activities. These end users have been determined to present an unacceptable risk of diversion to developing weapons of mass destruction or the missiles used to deliver those weapons.
4. Embargoed Countries List, U.S. Department of Commerce, issued by the Bureau of Export Administration.
5. International Traffic in Arms Debarment List, issued by the Department of State, includes individuals convicted of conspiracy/violations of the Arms Export Control Act, who now are subject to statutory debarment from participating in arms export transactions.
6. Sanctions List, Department of State, Office of Foreign Assets.

How Do I Use the Results?

Should a match occur, the requested transaction would be stopped before execution. It is recommended that a customer service agent review the order before any communication is sent to the customer or the product is shipped.

Building This In-House

You can easily build a system to check for these addresses yourself. Just remember you have to constantly look for updates and make sure they are loaded into your system.
For More Information on Recent Export Regulation News:
http://www.cnn.com/2001/US/09/24/ret.bush.transcript/index.html
For complete details on the Executive Order issued September 24, 2001:
http://www.ustrea.gov/ofac/
http://www.bxa.doc.gov/

Chapter 22

E-Commerce Insurance

Merchants use e-commerce insurance to cover their losses on orders that are fraudulent.

How Good Is It?

Insurance has been around for a long time, and e-commerce insurance certainly does work. However like any other form of insurance, these companies are in business to make money, so their costs can be extensive, and the orders that are covered may be limited.

- Can be very costly for what you get.
- May require you to set up elaborate fraud-prevention techniques on top of the insurance.
- Can also affect sales conversion by forcing you to only accept orders that are on the bottom of the risk pile. For example you can only accept order when AVS is a full match.

Considerations When Implementing or Buying This Functionality

- Are all goods and services covered by the policy?
- What is the notification process? What types of information need to be collected and provided for a claim?
- Does the policy require that the merchant perform collection activities?
- How will future premiums be affected by losses?

Estimated Costs – Typically these services are offered on a basis points system. You will be required to pay a half to five basis points for the insurance on each order you want covered.

Alternative Solutions – Some fraud providers offer guarantees and risk sharing. Some fraud techniques offer guarantees as well, such as the Visa Verified by Visa Program, the MasterCard SecureCode offering and the American Express Advanced Address Verification Service.

Vendors – Start with your merchant business insurance provider.

How Does it Work?

Merchants will enter into an agreement with an underwriter that will require them to pay a preset basis point rate for each order they desire to have insured. Merchants will probably be required to have certain fraud-prevention techniques in place. These could be based on the standard association fraud tools such as AVS and card security schemes, but could also include the use of hot lists, fraud-screening services and/or the use of financial limits. Typically these policies will classify merchants by levels of risk based on the cost of their goods sold, the type of goods sold, and the fraud-prevention tools you have in place.

How Do I Use the Results?

The best practice with e-commerce insurance is to combine it with a broader strategy in which you use the insurance for those orders you would normally review, or on those orders that are in the gray area (i.e., not really good, but not really bad). The intent again is to automate the process, so this assumes if a merchant takes out insurance on all orders they would normally review, that they aren't reviewing these orders now that they have insurance.

Building This In-House

N/A

Chapter 23

Fraud Scoring

Fraud Scoring is used by merchants to determine the level of risk associated with taking an order in the card-not-present marketplace. Merchants use the score either to reject, review or accept orders, as well as to find out information on what other types of preventive checks they should perform on the order.

How Good Is It?

Use of fraud scoring services gives merchants a much more economical way to use the effectiveness of external checks that could be costly to implement individually; such as delivery address verification, geolocation, credit checks, reverse lookups, shared negative files, cross-merchant velocity and use of neural nets. It also frees the merchant up from training, setting up and maintaining an internal neural network or fraud solution.

An internal fraud scoring system will only have limited effectiveness, as the breadth of data that is being looked at is only a single merchant's data. This will affect any and all velocity checks such as velocity of change and velocity of use. For example, modeling and neural nets that are built, and/or used, solely in a one-merchant implementation don't get the benefit of seeing consumer activity outside of their business. For fraud scoring the more data that go into building the service, the better it will predict and catch fraud.

It is important to know that:

- Modeling and neural nets that are maintained in-house suffer from breadth of data, missing key information from attempts on cross-merchant data.

- Better fraud-screening services will catch between 40% and 70% of fraud attempts, but the higher the catch rate the higher the insult rate.
- It is only a tool: It provides good information, but merchants have to build the logic into their system to handle the responses.
- It can be very difficult to set up and understand how to effectively weight rules if building in-house. Can require significant intellectual capital.
- It is a great tool to automate manual fraud reviews.

Considerations When Implementing or Buying This Functionality

- How often are the underlying models updated? This is important as the fraud patterns and data points that are used in a model come from actual good and bad purchases. If a model is a year old, merchants are trying to predict fraud off of data elements that were fraud that occurred a year ago, whereas a model updated monthly or on every transaction is looking at more recent patterns.
- How often is the data updated and verified by the vendor?
- What types of fraud-prevention techniques does the vendor use (e.g., heuristics, neural nets, external scores)?
- What other components does the service provider include as part of their screening service (e.g., delivery address verification, reverse lookups, geolocation, freight forwarder checks)?
- Do they offer any guarantee on charge-backs or provide any risk sharing?
- Do they offer a pass/fail-only solution or one that provides a true score and range?
- Does the fraud-scoring service support e-commerce, mail order and telephone order? Remember to look at the data elements they use to confirm what the focus of the service is. A service designed to predict e-commerce fraud will have less effectiveness in detecting mail order and telephone order fraud, as the data elements are different. For example the e-commerce consumer will have an IP number and e-mail address.
- For merchants that do a lot of volume, this solution can get very expensive, so make sure you negotiate volume discounts.
- What case studies can they give to show how effective the solution was for other merchants?

- Be leery of any fraud-scoring service that guarantees less than .5% fraud without explaining what the effect will be on sales conversion.
- One direct measure of the depth of a fraud-screening service is the number of descriptors it can relate back to help you understand why it scored the way it did. These are codes that tell you more about why it scored they way it did (e.g., can't verify address, geolocation inconsistency with country, high velocity of use, currently on a negative list).
- What type of reports does the service provide?
- Does the service provide tools for the fraud-review team to do manual reviews?
- Can a merchant tune or change the service to meet their unique needs?
- Can they tell you what to expect as far as insult rates?
- If the service offers negative files, are these shared negative files or strictly for the merchant putting in the data?

Estimated Costs – Costs will vary based on the vendor you select. Typically this service is offered on a transaction basis. There are some providers that offer flat subscription pricing, volume discounts and better pricing for entering long-term agreements. There are also some providers that offer basis points pricing, and these typically offer some sort of risk sharing or charge-back guarantee.

Alternative Solutions – Use of a decision engine, application of rules.

Vendors – CyberSource, Clear Commerce, Mango, Experian, Equifax, Fair Isaac/HNC, Lightbridge, Lexis-Nexis (Riskwise), ChoicePoint, TrustMarque Risk Guardian, Retail Decisions. CyberSource has a unique relationship and development arrangement with Visa, offering a solution that is enhanced and endorsed by Visa. CyberSource is unique in the fraud-scoring market space with its Visa relationship.

How Does it Work?

First a merchant must understand that they can either use an external service for fraud scoring or they can build their own fraud-scoring engine. In general you will send an order to a fraud-scoring service, which will provide all of the data elements of the order. Typically the merchant will have performed an authorization prior to making this call, so they can provide information such as address verification results and the card security results to the fraud-scoring service. These services are typically set up to process orders in a real-time environment, but this does not mean a merchant can't use them in a batch mode. The service typically takes a matter of seconds to evaluate an order to determine the level of risk associated with it. Once a fraud-scoring service is done, it will provide one of several data points back to the merchant. Make sure to check what the service provider will return:

A pass or fail result
A score
Descriptors

So now that you understand what you will see, what is the fraud-scoring service doing with their order? When you call a fraud-scoring service it runs a series of data integrity checks on the data you provided to look for things that are unusual or are blatantly fraudulent. Examples of this could be nonsensical input such as: Name: IUYIOUYIY, or it could be that "Mickey Mouse" is trying to buy a brand new three caret diamond ring. The service can then look at the data elements (such as name, address, phone, e-mail) to see if there are any matches to internal fraud lists. It would then check for issues with velocity of use and change. The service may then look at things such as geolocation, address and phone verification, and combine these in a model to see how well this order compares to previous good and bad orders. The service then correlates this into a score or a pass/fail response. This is only an example. Each service is unique, and most vendors will not share the exact methods they use, as this is their "secret sauce."

How Do I Use the Results?

Selecting a fraud-screening service depends on a merchant's sales channels, MOTO, e-commerce or both. If a fraud-screening service requires data elements from you, you should do everything you can to submit any and all of these data elements. E-commerce fraud-screening services will have less effectiveness with MOTO transactions. But if a solution is 70% effective in e-commerce and it is 50% effective with MOTO it will still catch half of the fraud attempts.

If an order fails authorization merchants don't need to send it out for fraud scoring. This being said a merchant should perform their authorization check prior to a fraud screen.

These services typically don't provide a case management interface, and they provide no means to establish initial settings. Merchants have to base the original settings off of their own previous history with charge-backs. Merchants can easily get bogged down in the details of the solution. I highly recommend that merchants have a fraud analyst from the vendor of choice or independent source to assist in completing the initial set up, going over best practices of using the fraud-screening service. This can save a merchant a lot of time and money in implementing their solution.

Building This In-House

It takes typically two weeks to set up a fraud-screening service technically: One week of setting up their initial business processes to use the service, and one week for completing the integration. Most vendors provide an API that has been designed to be very simple to use, and which has a lot of pre-built plug-ins to major e-commerce applications.
Implementing fraud screening is easy from a technical standpoint, but is a little trickier from the business side. You need to do a fair amount of analysis on your side to determine what types of risk may be encountered. Also a merchant has to determine how they want to deal with that risk. This information is critical for correctly setting up and using fraud scoring to its fullest potential. Merchants will also have to code in rules to handle return results from fraud-scoring services.

Chapter 24

Freight Forwarders

The intent of using freight forwarder checks is to ensure the shipping address where goods are being delivered is not a freight forwarder that may be shipping the goods or services to other destinations.

How Good Is It?

Typically the freight forwarder check is used to make sure the goods or services you are providing are not being reshipped to a third party via freight forwarder. Fraudsters outside the U.S. like to use these freight forwarder services to make it look like they are coming from within the United States.

- There is a lot of inherent risk for goods and services being delivered to freight forwarder.
- Good tool to catch international fraudsters masking themselves as U.S. companies.

Considerations When Implementing or Buying This Functionality

- How will the list of freight forwarders be compiled? Will the merchant try to compile it, or will they use an external service to provide this information?
- Does their service keep any data on fraud found with a particular freight forwarder?
- How often is their service updated with new numbers?

Estimated Costs – Typically this service is offered on a per-transaction basis, but you can also purchase it as a subscription. There are some very low cost providers online, that have hosted screens for you to input data manually as well. This service is usually fairly inexpensive.

Alternative Solutions – Fraud Scoring solution that includes this capability, Delivery Address Verification Service that provides associated phone data with an address. Do geolocation validation on the zip code or area code.

Vendors – First Logic, Group One, Acxiom, InfoUSA

How Does it Work?

If using it as a manual tool, you would enter the shipping address and phone information into a hosted screen or utility the IT shop has set up for the merchant. The service or application would come back with a response to indicate if the address was a freight forwarder or not.

How Do I Use the Results?

Don't be surprised if the phone number does not match for the address given, this will happen a lot where the fraudster uses a separate number to reach them, and the address of a freight forwarder for the goods.

This is a good tool to use with tools that provide geolocation data. If the consumer's geolocation information on the IP address showed he was from outside the U.S. and the address and phone data showed that he was inside the U.S. and the address is listed as a freight forwarder, you probably have a fraudster. Make sure to hot list addresses of freight forwarders when you do get a fraud attempt or charge-back from their address and/or phone number.

Building This In-House

Try to automate the lookup for freight forwarders, as it is easy to do, and if you use it with geolocation it can save you a lot of manual reviews.

Chapter 25

Geolocation

Geolocation services provide detailed information about a consumer's worldwide location, line speed, domain, etc. It is used primarily to verify the consumer's data to determine where the consumer is at the time of purchase. Geolocation Services can be used for fraud prevention and also used for export and regulatory compliance.

For Fraud Prevention - Geolocation shows a merchant if the consumer is trying to hide their identity. For example, it flags the result if they are making the purchase from a location that is vastly different from the billing or shipping information. A consumer gives the merchant an address and phone number in New York but the IP address is showing that the consumer is coming from Russia.

For Regulatory Compliance - For industries such as gaming, digital software download, and certain export industries, they would use this service to validate that the consumer is really in the location they say they are in. They can also ensure that they don't provide goods or services to consumers in countries where it may be prohibited.

How Good Is It?

In general these services are pretty reliable and they offer a valuable tool for merchants. The best application for this tool is in the regulatory compliance arena. For fraud prevention it provides a valuable tool but cannot stand alone in making a decision to accept or reject an order. Purchasing this solution can be more expensive than most fraud-scoring services, which typically provide this type of a check as part of the scoring service.

Pros and cons of geolocation include:

- Easy to implement.
- Best method to validate regulatory compliance on country.
- Only useful when you have an IP address, so it will not work for other card-not-present transactions such as phone-based orders.
- Good for catching large discrepancies between the data provided and the actual location of the consumer, but due to the nature of the web and people traveling, merchants do have to be careful about how they implement this as a fraud-prevention tool. In general, if a merchant only does business in a certain country, this is a great tool to catch those consumers from outside the country before they get into the order-processing stream.

Considerations When Implementing or Buying This Functionality

- Can the solution see through proxies and through services such as AOL to determine where an order is coming from?
- Can the solution tell how reliable the information is when you get it? For example, level of confidence by country or region?
- What other types of data does the service provide as part of the solution such as: Geographic information: Continent, Country, Time Zone, State, City, Zip, Area Code, Longitude/Latitude, DMA, MSA, PMSA. Proxy Information such as AOL, Anonymous Proxies, Cache Proxies, Corporate Proxies. Network information. Domain Name, Network Connection type, Network Speed, Autonomous System Number, Backbone Carrier Name?
- How often is the data updated and verified by the vendor?

Estimated Costs – Costs will vary based on the vendor you select. Nslookup, Whereis and Whois are utilities that provide this information in a basic form for free. You can also find vendors that offer more sophisticated services as in-house software solutions with subscription fees, or on a completely outsourced model with a per-transaction fee.

Alternative Solutions – You can also look at trying some of the Fraud-Scoring Services that offer the Geolocation check as part of the score.

Vendors – CyberSource, Clear Commerce, Quova, Digital Envoy, Akamai, SamSpade.org

How Does it Work?

Geolocation services provide detailed information about a consumer's worldwide location, line speed, domain, etc. These services rely on the IP address. Merchants can get the IP address from the HTTP header on the order that comes into their site. This IP address can be compared to the location the consumer says he or she is at and a determination can be made if the order is fraudulent or not.

Geolocation services can offer a variety of information at varying degrees of depth, but the information can be lumped into three major categories:

1. Geographic information, such as continent, country, time zone, state, city, zip, area code, longitude/latitude, DMA, MSA, PMSA
2. Proxy information, such as AOL, Anonymous Proxies, Cache Proxies, Corporate Proxies.
3. Network information, such as domain name, network connection type, network speed, autonomous system number and backbone carrier name.

The value of looking at the proxy information is that proxy servers can hide the actual location of a consumer. If a consumer is using a proxy server on the West Coast of the United States and they live on the East Coast, their IP address will make you think they are coming from the opposite coast from where they actually are.

This same ability to hide where they are coming from can also be used by potential fraudsters in Asia or Europe to make it look like they are coming from the United States. Anonymous Proxies were intended for privacy reasons so users could mask where they are coming from. AOL consumers are one of the biggest issues in determining where the consumer really is, because they all look like they are coming from Virginia.

Tip: Make sure your provider is using a technology that can dig out a consumer's location even through proxies and services such as AOL. Quova is one of the services that can dig out the consumer location even when they are AOL users.

Many vendors offer geolocation services, but many have not created their own solutions and are actually using the technology of a handful of technology providers like Quova.

The core of an IP Geolocation service is the mapping of IP addresses to global locations to create a global data collection network. The system, provided by Quova, uses multiple automated techniques and algorithms to collect, map and analyze the billions of IP addresses that make up the Internet, plus international teams of expert analysts to review the data, refining and developing new, more powerful algorithms. This unique combination of processing power from a large collection network and analysis from human experts allows the system to accurately keep up with the Internet's complexity and rapid rate of change. The result is levels of data quality and accuracy that are unsurpassed and constantly improving.

How Do I Use the Results?

In using a geolocation service merchants can feel more confident in accepting orders in which the IP address geolocation check matches up with the "ship to" or "bill to" address.

In using a geolocation service, if merchants find a major discrepancy with the IP geolocation match to the "ship to" or "bill to" address then you should review or decline the order.

If the geolocation service provider gives the merchant country or city information, the merchant can create rules to decline these orders for regions they do not do business in. They can also prevent business in regions where they have had a high incidence of fraud in the past.

If the geolocation service provider gives a merchant information about proxies, the merchant can build rules to do further fraud screening for orders in which anonymous proxies and cache proxies are evident.

If a merchant runs the geolocation service on every transaction and stores the data results, the merchant can build a very targeted marketing profile of their customer base, including demographics on region, time of day and methods of getting to their site.

Building This In-House

There are several methods a merchant can use to build their own geolocation capability in-house. Building these types of services in-house means they have to be committed to maintaining them going forward, which can be extensive.

- Area Code Check – Using a phone book, build out a list of all area codes by state and set up a rule to check the area code given with the phone number to the state of billing and/or shipping address. If they don't match, review or reject the order.

- Zip Code Check – Using commercially available mailing services, build a list of all zip codes by state and country, and set up a rule to check to see if the data matches.
- IP Address Check – Using freeware services available online such as BigIP, check the incoming IP address to see where it is coming from. A merchant must have a listing showing where these addresses reside. This has a lot of issues, as proxies and services such as AOL will mask a lot of the transaction's real origins.
- Credit Card Bin Check – Create rules to weed out orders coming from the same credit card bin range with non-matching geolocation data. Look for the same credit card bin range with deliveries being billed to a specific city, state, or zip code.

Chapter 26

Guaranteed Payments

Guaranteed payments are the use of a third party to provide a merchant with a guarantee of payment for fraudulent transactions. These include providers of e-commerce insurance, third-party fraud services, and consumer authentication schemes.

How Good Is It?

This is the holy grail of solutions: Merchants are guaranteed that the charge-back will be covered, so it works great. Not every charge-back is guaranteed, only fraud charge-backs are covered; merchants still have to deal with customer service charge-backs. These solutions will have the right of refusal, or require you to provide some stringent data requirements for them to guarantee the purchase. This is not a cheap option, and you will pay for the guarantee, but if a merchant's margins are low and they need to make sure they don't get hit from fraud, this is one of the best ways to do so.

Note that with guaranteed payments:

- Not all charge-backs are guaranteed, only those that are fraud-based, no guarantee on customer service charge-backs.
- It usually works only for a specific card type, such as Visa or MasterCard.
- It may only work for specific channels, such as e-commerce or MOTO.
- Providers reserve right of refusal, so it can adversely impact sales conversion.

Considerations When Implementing or Buying This Functionality

- Make sure to take time to understand what level of insult rates you will have with the solution. For example, if they guarantee only when they process the order and say yes, how many of the ones they said no to will actually be good orders.
- What channels do they support (e.g., e-commerce, MOTO)?
- Does it require anything extra from their consumer to process the order?
- What credit cards do they support?

Estimated Costs – Low to Very Expensive. Typically involves paying basis points on top of the order. The consumer authentication techniques, Verified by Visa and MasterCard SecureCode are very inexpensive.

Alternative Solutions – Using fraud-scoring services that offer risk sharing.

Vendors – Visa – Verified by Visa, MasterCard – SecureCode, American Express – Advanced Address Verification and Paymentech – VerifyME

How Does it Work?

For all of the guaranteed payment solutions, except e-commerce insurance, merchants will provide the order information to the vendor. The vendor will evaluate the order data, perform screening and provide them with an answer to accept or reject. Depending on the provider they choose, they may not state that the order is guaranteed.

Merchants have to set up processes that follow all of the vendor's rules to get the orders guaranteed. For example in the consumer authentication techniques the merchant will pass an ID with the order showing they got the authentication, but that alone does not mean they're covered. They still have to be following all of the other rules with the program. For instance, marking the transaction correctly, no selling of prohibited products or services, such as gambling or adult content.

How Do I Use the Results?

How you use the results is directly related to the program requirements. Make sure all requirements are being following exactly as listed and document all of the required elements they ask for. It is their choice to accept or reject with most of these services, but if a merchant does accept when they said no to them, the merchant is on their own.

Building This In-House

Start with the consumer authentication schemes — they are the cheapest ways to get a guarantee. Then move to the Advanced Address Verification technique. And then finally, if the other techniques are not enough, look for a third party to provide guarantees on goods and services or look for e-commerce insurance.

Chapter 27

Hot Lists, Warm Lists and Positive Lists

Lists are used to identify returning consumers to determine if they have had good business or bad business in the past. Hot lists, sometimes referred to as negative lists, are utilized to reject orders from consumers that have had charge-backs on previous orders. Warm lists are used to either reject or review orders from consumers who have been customer-satisfaction problems in the past. Warm lists aren't used for fraudsters, just consumers that never seem to be satisfied. Positive lists are used to identify a merchant's best customers who have successfully closed business with them in the past and are trying to make a new purchase.

How Good Is It?

The use of lists is one of the most fundamental elements in any fraud-prevention strategy. If a merchant is doing nothing today, implementing a hot list is the very first thing they should do. If a merchant is doing business today and someone defrauds them, and the merchant has nothing in place to prevent the fraudster from coming back and defrauding them again, the fraudster will come back. Lists in general can also save a company money by allowing them to cut out certain orders before they have to pay for external calls such as authorizations, fraud screening, credit checks and the like.

Things to know about lists are:

- Hot lists are excellent at preventing repeat fraud, and are fairly good at catching some forms of identity morphing.

- Warm lists are an effective way to stop those customers that continuously make purchases and then just return the goods, or don't make full payments.
- Warm lists are also a good way to track return or credit abuse.
- Positive lists are an excellent way to reduce the number of orders you have to call out to external fraud screening for. They are also a good way to fast-track orders from a merchant's best customers if they rely heavily on manual reviews.

Considerations When Implementing or Buying This Functionality

- To maximize the effectiveness of using lists, a merchant should make sure they can share data from, and be checked from all channels (i.e., e-commerce, MOTO and card-present) if possible.
- Merchants can exponentially increase the effectiveness of lists by having access to shared fraud lists.
- The data fields a merchant uses for these lists are critical, so make sure you can add data elements, import and export data into the set. Also make sure you have methods to purge old records.
- Plan on maintaining data in a hot list for at least 12 months — I recommend 18 months.

Estimated Costs – Costs vary based on the method you implement. A merchant can get basic hot list capabilities from most fraud-screening services, and they can get it as part of most decision engines. They can also build it internally very easily.

Alternative Solutions – None

Vendors – CyberSource, Clear Commerce, Retail Decisions, HNC/Fair Isaac

How Does it Work?

List checks are fairly simple: A merchant designates a set of fields to maintain in a database, and they populate it with records where they want to take some action. When they process a transaction, they check it against the list.

Typically the data element used for list checks are address, state, zip code, phone number, credit card number and e-mail address. Name is not recommended as there are too many people with similar names and this could really kill their sales or fill their manual review bins.

When checking new transactions against the database, a merchant is looking for a match on any of the data elements, not just one of them. For address checks merchants will have to use some normalization to be effective. Make sure states are represented in the two-character designation, zip codes are five digits or five-plus-four and all blanks are stripped out of the address line. Look for matches on parts of the address line, not exact matches, as some individuals will change just one digit or letter to make it look like a different address. Set up a process that mandates that all charge-backs that are related to fraud must be input into the hot list.

How Do I Use the Results?

- Always perform the hot list check first, before any call for an authorization. If a consumer is on the hot list, reject the order.
- If using warm lists to catch customer service issues, do this check second, before authorization. If a merchant's policy is to reject all warm list customers simply cancel the order, otherwise if it is to review, then do this check after you do the authorization.
- Positive file checks, unlike the warm list or hot list, must be a 100% match. Address, phone and e-mail — everything — must match before a merchant decides to skip any other fraud checks.

One of the interesting ways warm lists have been implemented is to catch customers that are constantly returning goods. They can also be used to catch internal fraud rings that do credits to third-party credit cards. The method calls for a connection to their applications that process credits. Using a velocity of use technique, they count the number of credits based on each of the data elements discussed earlier. When they reach a preset number (e.g., more than 3 in 30 days), have that data populated into the warm list.

Building This In-House

The main thing a merchant needs is a database. Have a Database Administrator set up a database to use, adding the data elements discussed above. Working with the credit or finance group, compile a list of previous charge-backs using the data elements to fill it in. You can put the data into a comma-separated file or you can put it into a spreadsheet application such as Microsoft Excel. With the spreadsheet or comma-separated file, the Database Administrator should be able to easily import the data into the database.

The next step is to set up a call to the database from the e-commerce engine, if a merchant is processing orders in real time, or from their order-processing application if they are operating in batch. The Database Administrator can set up the lists so they are optimized for fast queries by presetting stored procedures. Remember, although it is easy to add this directly to the e-commerce engine, I recommend that you create a fraud-prevention strategy first and implement this and other techniques with the end-state "strategy" in mind.

Chapter 28

Internal Rules

Internal rules are built into e-commerce engines, payment processing systems or order management systems to attempt to catch potentially risky orders. Sometime called "heuristics," these are simple logic statements that look to see if a condition is present.

They usually take the form of pass/fail, true/false or yes/no type of questions, and are normally used to find risky or "negative" conditions. It doesn't have to be that way, but that is the typical application approach.

How Good Is It?

In writing rules you must remember that it is only natural to tend to write them to catch risky behavior. If you attempt to only write rules that are based on previous fraud attempts you will find that your risk solution, and catch rules, will be relative in nature, causing you to have to put in fixes and updates regularly. Be proactive in building rules — look at and profile good orders and base rules on that behavior to let these orders flow freely.

Other things to know about rules:

- Rules form the basis for heuristics and catching negative characteristics of orders.
- With a well thought out strategy, rules can offer the lowest cost solution to keep fraud losses in check.
- Most manual checks can be implemented as rules.
- Within the rules discussion I have not discussed building rules based on other fraud technique tools such as card security, AVS, hot list or velocity as these rules and techniques are discussed in their own sections.

Considerations When Implementing or Buying This Functionality

- Implementing rules requires a merchant to keep a good overview of the intended overall strategy. This will ensure they don't create more work for themselves by creating rules that cause them to review more orders than they really need to.
- Rules should be based on quantitative data, so make sure that you can prove that the majority of the transactions the rule will weed out really are fraudulent.
- Make sure only one entity is responsible for adding, changing or deleting rules, to ensure multiple parties in a business are not canceling each other's rules out.
- Make sure checks are done consistently.
- A lot of e-commerce engines have some built-in ability to add rules, such as the "pipeline" object in the Microsoft e-commerce platform.

Estimated Costs – Implementing rules in-house is very inexpensive to do. You can have an internal resource directly code the rules in, or you can hire a third party to input the rules. Merchants can purchase commercially available decisioning software that will allow them to build rule logic.

Alternative Solutions – Use of third-party service to build a custom set of rules for a merchant.

Vendors – CyberSource, Clear Commerce, Retail Decision, HNC Fair Isaac

How Does it Work?

- Dollar Amount – Reject or review all orders over an order amount of $X. This is a dangerous rule, as most fraud rings will work a merchant site to determine what this threshold is and will submit orders just below that. The merchant moves their threshold, and then the fraudsters move theirs. To be effective this rule cannot be under the average order amount for the business or within 15% of the average. The amount rule should be coupled with other rules such as shipping type, product type, quantity or region.
- Shipping Type – looks at order to see if overnight or express shipping has been requested. In itself this does not indicate fraud

but in conjunction with other rules, it does and it can indicate higher risk.

- Product Type Rule – Set up a list of SKUs, product names or codes that are for high risk items, things routinely stolen or have a high incidence of theft.
- Quantity Rule – Set up a rule to catch orders in which unusual numbers of items are being ordered, for example more than one laptop or more than two CD's of the same type.
- Regional Rule – Set up a rule to catch orders that are from a high-risk region of the country (e.g., NY, FL, CA or down to the city level).
- International Rule – Set up a rule to catch all orders that are not from a desired country by looking at shipping, billing address, card bin or geolocation check.
- Different Billing & Shipping Addresses – Set up a rule to catch all orders in which the billing and shipping address are different.
- Profanity Rule – Set up a rule to review all text input fields, especially name, address, and e-mail to check for profanity (e.g., "fuck," "damn," "bitch," "bastard" and "ass"). These are not typically found in real names or addresses and indicate high risk.
- No Vowels Rule – Set up a rule that looks at addresses, e-mail, and names to check for gibberish no "a, e, i, o, u, y" characters. It is very rare for this to occur. Merchants can also vary this to check for more than six consonant with no vowels.
- Famous Names Rule – Early fraud online used famous names or common names to perpetrate a crime. Create a list to check against this such as John Wayne, Marilyn Monroe, John and Jane Doe. Not a dead indicator of fraud but I would check twice if Mickey Mouse was ordering ten CD's.
- Card Security Number Rule – If a merchant is taking in the card security number, they can perform a quick test on the numbers the consumer provides to them to look for suspicious patterns. This check is very important if a merchant is collecting the card security number and isn't actually checking it. Look for "000," "001," "123" and "111" these are all highly suspicious numbers for the Card Security number, if a merchant has the ability to do velocity of change checking on additional data fields, perform a velocity of change check on the card security number as well.

- Home-Built Area Code Rule - Using your phone book, build a list of all area codes by state and set up a rule to check the area code given with the phone number to the state of billing and/or shipping address. If they don't match, review or reject the order.
- Private Mailboxes - In the past, crooks have used mail drop locations such as Mail Boxes, Etc., as delivery points for goods ordered fraudulently by telephone or the Internet. Such a delivery address might appear as though it were a business:

TO:

John Doe
My Company
123 Any Street, Suite 333
Mytown, State ZIP

Recently the U.S. Postal Service established a requirement that mail-drop addresses be identified as such. Effective April 2000, the Postal Service may refuse to deliver to private mail drop locations unless the mailbox is included in the address and identified as "PMB." The preceding address would then be legitimately displayed as:

TO:

John Doe
My Company
123 Any Street, PMB 333
Mytown, State ZIP

- Business Hour Check - Create a rule to check the time of day for the order in the geographic zone the order is coming from and see if it matches the normal business hours. Business hours can be extended hours, but the thing you are looking to do is see if an order is being placed at 2am in the area the person is placing the order from. Then decide if that makes sense when you look at their typical customers. Typical time envelopes are 8am to 5pm, 6am to 8pm, 6am to 11pm and 11pm to 6am.

How Do I Use the Results?

There are three accepted methods of utilizing rules within a strategy:
1. Rule list - Merchants implement their rules as a set of checks with each one indicating fail or review. If any one condition comes up true, the list is stopped and the result is returned as review or fail. Typically all fail conditions are put at the top of the list with review

conditions put afterwards. On the plus side, this is the easiest method to implement. On the negative side, merchants only get one return value so they don't know if multiple conditions failed or required review.

2. Weighted List – Merchants implement a set of rules, with each rule having a weighted score for true or false. A score range is established and within the range sub-ranges are set for pass, fail and review. On the plus side, they can mix positive and negative factors and get quite sophisticated with scoring. On the negative side, this requires a lot of research and maintenance to ensure it doesn't hurt sales. It typically has a longer learning curve.

3. Decision Tree – Merchants implement a set of rules that follow a path based on each preceding rule. For example, if condition A is true then do this, if not then do that.

Building This In-House

Building an in-house rules engine is very easy to do, and most merchants have implemented some form of rule engine already. It is recommended that, unless a merchant has a fairly sophisticated technical group, they use a commercially available rules engine to implement rules. This ensures that they can easily see what rules have been put into place and it allows them to ensure that the solution is being maintained from someone other than their internal resources.

Chapter 29

Manual Review

Manual review is a technique in which merchants use staff members to perform manual checks on orders to determine which orders are fraudulent.

How Good Is It?

In general, this is not a very good fraud-prevention technique. The quality and effectiveness of manual reviews is directly proportional to the knowledge and experience of the review staff, and the tools and process that they have established to perform manual reviews.

According to a merchant survey conducted by CyberSource Corporation in 2002, more than 50% of the merchants surveyed use some level of manual review and they were reviewing between 16% and 28% of the total number of orders they were processing. The survey also shows that the more sales the merchant did, the more likely they were to be using some sort of manual review.

This represents a big issue when it comes to scalability. If merchants are relying on manual review, what do they do when their business grows or when they have peaks? As a quick fix, or as a tool to look at for sales conversion, manual reviews are very effective. When it comes to fraud prevention, merchants need to be very careful how much they rely on them.

If merchants are going to rely on manual reviews, they need to use it to review the orders they were going to reject anyway. This allows merchants to have the possibility of converting an "insult" instead of trying to catch fraudulent orders.

Drawbacks of manual reviews include:
- It does not scale well, the only way to grow is to add new staff.

- The more people doing reviews the more unpredictable the results, as each will have varying levels of experience and will adopt their own styles for looking for fraud.
- There are good reasons to do manual reviews, but it should be done to catch those orders a merchant wants to try and keep instead of trying to find fraudulent orders.
- It typically lacks formal training of reviewers.

Considerations When Implementing or Buying This Functionality

- How many orders can their reviewers process?
- How much time will it add to their process?
- What percentage of fraud do they have to catch to make up the difference in their pay?
- How many customers will be falsely rejected by the process (insults)?
- What tools will be provided to the team to conduct the manual reviews?

Estimated Costs – Moderate to expensive

Alternative Solutions – Rules engine, fraud scoring, hot lists, warm lists, positive lists and consumer authentication

Vendors – N/A

How Does it Work?

Merchants set up a fraud-review team. Typically this team will work under the Call Center or the Finance Department. This team will be charged with reviewing all of the company's orders to determine which ones are fraudulent.

The team may have built sorts or queries that put the order data into views in which they can look for suspicious activity. They may look at activity by region, credit card number, or order size. In some cases they will have queues built to provide them with the orders that need to be reviewed.

When the team finds a suspect order, they may simply reject the order or they may do follow up to try and determine if the order is good. Some of the common tools used in conducting a manual review are:

- Call the bank and verify the shipping and billing information
- Use a lookup tool to check the consumer's address and phone information
- Check historical purchase records to see if there is any other activity from this consumer in the past
- Call and verify the order data with the consumer
- Have the consumer fax or mail in copies of their driver's license, a utility bill from the address, and/or credit card statement

How Do I Use the Results?

As a best practice, it is a very effective way to maximize sales to set up automated processes to weed out the orders a merchant would not automatically accept, and then use reviews on what is remaining. This also allows a merchant to scale better, since they are only reviewing orders they were going to reject anyway.

Building This In-House

N/A

Chapter 30

MasterCard SecureCode

MasterCard SecureCode is an emerging tool that is intended to validate that the authorized credit card holder is the one actually attempting to make a purchase. Visa has a similar service called Verified by Visa.

How Good Is It?

In general the concept of authenticating the consumer is a good one. For the merchant, this is an excellent tool because it is one of the first tools that actually offers some financial coverage if fraud does occur. The card associations implemented these programs to increase consumer confidence in making purchases online and to help protect online merchants from fraud.

The main reason a merchant wants to implement this service is the protection it offers from fraud-related charge-backs. Not everything is protected, so make sure to review the details of the program with MasterCard. There are significant differences on what is covered in the U.S. versus what is covered in Europe. Some examples of what is not covered by the program include: purchases made with procurement cards, recurring billing, split shipments or back-ordered goods, "one-click" technology sales and transactions in which the consumer cannot be authenticated.

They are introducing some workarounds for things, such as backordered goods and split shipments. Make sure to check and see what updates have been made to the rules and regulations when they implement the service.

It also seems that certain high-risk segments, such as adult and gaming, are not going to be covered. So if you are in these vertical markets you should check before you buy. There is no threshold set for risk, but there is wording that suggests that a threshold for fraud rates may be set and a merchant will have to keep their losses below that. Also merchants have to properly set the e-commerce-preferred indicator.

The other major benefit of the MasterCard SecureCode technique is the simplification of some of their charge-back resolution activities. For those orders in which the consumer was participating in the program and a merchant did authenticate them, the resolution process would occur between the issuing bank and the consumer, not between the merchant and the consumer.

Consumers may be legitimate even if they can't authenticate. Some examples of reasons why good customers may not be able to authenticate include:

- the use of software the prevents pop-up windows will render this service obsolete,
- the pop-up can time out or
- consumers that were pre-registered may not know they have a password or PIN to use this.

Considerations When Implementing or Buying This Functionality

- Works only on e-commerce transactions. Merchants have to have fraud processes to handle their MOTO traffic.
- The merchant, consumer, issuer and acquiring bank must all be participating in the program. So make sure their acquiring bank is set up to support the e-commerce indicator, and check on their certification requirements.
- For European merchants, some of the acquiring banks are still not set up to support consumer authentication.
- Merchants still need to perform other fraud checks. This tool does not cover many of the card types on the market today and there are legitimate cases in which a merchant may not be able to complete the authentication process with the consumer. Merchants also need to make sure their overall fraud rates are kept within standards. Also the industry expects some fraud shift to cards not offering this service.
- Companies doing little transactional volume should consider using an outsourced service bureau to perform this service.

- Make sure you are checking and providing all of the correct data points: Merchants have to mark transactions as e-commerce with the ECI, and they must check AVS, enrollment, and they need the CAVV/AVV, which shows the order was checked for enrollment. Merchants also need the XID (the unique transaction number).
- Merchants will have to get a digital certificate from MasterCard, which takes about two weeks. See the acquiring bank to get the form and start the process.

Estimated Costs – Merchants can find this service available as an outsourced service, or as a software application that can be implemented in-house. The actual cost to purchase the software is fairly low – a couple of thousand dollars to purchase. Merchants will have to pay annual maintenance on the software. Merchants will have to make changes to their front-end e-commerce engine.

Alternative Solutions – None

Vendors – Arcot, CyberSource, Clear Commerce

How Does it Work?

The process used by MasterCard SecureCode to authenticate consumers is pretty simple. The consumer enrolls with the issuing bank and is given a password, PIN or device to authenticate him or her. When the consumer makes a purchase online, the consumer is asked to give that password, PIN or device to authenticate.

The purchase sequence can be broken down into five stages. First the consumer goes through the checkout procedure the same way he or she does today, providing the same data fields. When he or she presses the buy button, the consumer's system, using the commercially available software on the market, sends a message to MasterCard to find out if the consumer is participating in the consumer authentication program. If the cardholder is participating in the program, MasterCard will send a pop-up window to the consumer. It appears as if the pop-up is coming from consumer's issuing bank, asking him or her to enter the password or PIN. The bank then validates this password or PIN and returns the results to the merchant.

For these programs to work, the merchant, consumer, issuer and acquiring bank must all be participating in the program. Consumer adoption is slow at best. Likewise merchant adoption has been slow. Merchant enrollment should increase over time.

Consumers are being enrolled by self-registration, issuer auto enrollment and issuer-prompted registration.

The liability shift is different based on the region the merchant is doing business in and the type of charge-back they have. For MasterCard only charge-backs coded as RC37 are covered right now. Currently for European transactions, in which the cardholder and merchant are European, they have the liability shift already.

From a security perspective, all communication between the consumer and issuing bank is secured. You as a merchant will not see or ask for this password. The pop-up window the end user receives contains a secret message that only the consumer knows, which shows the consumer that the pop-up window is real and not a fake that someone made to try and steal the password.

There was a fraud case in which fraudsters acquired account information and then called the issuing bank and changed the address information and signed up for Verified by Visa. The fraudsters then made a lot of fraudulent transactions. The merchants will be covered as long as they followed the rules.

How do I Use the Results?

For MasterCard orders when using this technology, you should implement the following:

- For orders in which the consumer is participating in the program, and the order type is a covered type, and the consumer successfully authenticates, accept the order.
- For orders in which the consumer is not participating in the program, and the order type is a covered type, you have checked for enrollment, and the order characteristics are within their normal order tolerances, accept the order.
- For orders in which the consumer is not participating in the program, and the order type is a covered type, you have checked for enrollment, and the order characteristics are not in-line with their normal orders, review the order or perform further fraud checks favoring sales conversion.
- For orders in which the consumer is participating in the program, and cannot successfully authenticate, and the order characteristics

are in-line with their normal orders, perform other fraud-screening checks or manually review the order favoring risk aversion.

- For non-Visa and MasterCard orders, perform traditional checks.

Building This In-House

Not Applicable.

Chapter 31

MOD 10 Check

The MOD 10 check takes the credit card number the customer submitted and validates that the number is in the correct range and format to be a credit card number and it is the type of credit card the consumer says it is.

How Good Is It?

When a consumer decides to buy on a site, the merchant is relying on them to input their information correctly the first time. If you think about this, it may seem simple, but in reality things do go wrong. Consumers could transpose numbers in the sequence, forget one of the digits, forget to input the expiration date or say it's a Visa card when it's really an American Express. These things slow down their order processing and clog up the system. And if you don't do anything to correct this information up front, you open yourself up to the most basic forms of attempted fraud by simply plugging numbers into their site.

Items to note about MOD 10 check:

- It does not tell you if it is active or not, just that it is in the correct format.
- This test is used on their website to validate that the credit card submitted is a recognizable credit card number.
- High – Helps to prevent you from processing credit card authorizations on numbers that could not possibly be credit cards.

The fact that someone gets their credit card number wrong on the buy page does not mean the order is fraudulent. They could have done any of a number of legitimate things to affect the information If someone repeatedly cannot pass through the MOD 10 check, then it is an issue.

Considerations When Implementing or Buying This Functionality

- Implement first — this is one of the lowest cost and easiest things to implement on your website, and you should implement it now if you are not using it already.
- Very easy to implement.
- Many development sites online offer free snippets of code for completing the MOD 10 Check.

Estimated Costs - No costs for doing the check, just the initial costs for setting up the code

Alternative Solutions - None

Vendors - None

How Does it Work?

The MOD 10 check is usually implemented right on the website in the web page that contains the buy button and credit card information. The code is a client-side script, so when the customer puts in their purchase information and presses the buy button the MOD 10 checks are done. The order is only sent to the merchant site when the MOD 10 check passes successfully. Implementing it this way saves you processing time to go back and forth with the consumer in the order processing. For merchants doing offline authorization it saves you manual intervention time, and call-backs. It also saves you money if you are paying each time you call for an authorization.

How Do I Use the Results?

Since it is a client-side script, you don't have to do anything with the results. You should not see a consumer order unless they can pass the MOD 10 check.

Building This In-House

1. Determine the proper code for your website.

2. Add the MOD 10 code to your customer order page on the submit button.

Chapter 32

Neural Nets

Neural nets are a form of modeling in which a computer attempts to predict good and positive outcomes by use of previous and current activity. Neural nets are not unique to fraud or fraud prevention; they are used in many different industries today. The neural net is typically the primary engine behind more sophisticated fraud-scoring applications.

How Good Is It?

Neural nets are very complicated to set up and maintain. They require very educated and experienced personnel to set up correctly. The value of a neural net is directly proportional to the people and data that went into making it. Generally speaking neural nets are very effective tools to predict risk.

The casual merchant is not going to go out and implement his or her own neural net solution. First, it is very expensive. Second, to build an effective neural net you need to have a lot of quality data to make sure it can accurately predict the positive and negative behavior.

- Requires very experienced and highly educated personnel to set up and maintain.
- Requires a lot of quality data, and must be refreshed often to be effective.

Considerations When Implementing or Buying This Functionality

- How often is the data in the neural net updated: per transaction, per quarter, semi annually or annually or greater?

- Where did the data inside the neural net come from? Did it come from the same type of sales channel you are using (for example, e-commerce, MOTO or card-present data)? Does it include data from multiple card types or mainly just one type?
- How many orders and how many other merchants or associations are feeding the data?

Estimated Costs - Very expensive

Alternative Solutions - Fraud scoring that offers neural nets modeling as part of their solution

Vendors - Fair Isaac

How Does it Work?

The neural net is based off of underlying models. These models attempt to make predictive correlations between data elements. For example, a correlation may be, "the more credit cards you see associated with an address the higher the risk." The neural net takes a bunch of these correlations. Then as an order is presented to the system it runs all of the correlation to come up with prediction about the outcome of the order.

In building a neural net you build a bunch of models and correlations and then you feed in a set of data to train the neural net. By training the neural net you are telling it the actual outcomes on known orders, and this becomes its basis for making future predictions. You are also showing the neural net how to weight certain correlations, since they are not all equal when it comes to predicting a desired outcome. This is why the quality and breadth of the data you use in your neural net is critical to accurately predict required outcomes.

Once you have trained a neural net, you have to test it with known test cases that you didn't feed into the model build in order to see how well it predicts the required outcome. Likewise you should do analysis at least once a quarter to determine the effectiveness of the predictions of the neural net.

Once the neural net is ready for actual use, it is typically set up to provide a ranged score (say, 1-100 or 1 to infinity) that indicates the level of risk with an order. Needless to say you also have to do analysis on the scores that get spit out of the neural net to understand what a score of 10 versus 10,000 really means to you.

Accumulating the required data, and making sure it is clean and accurate takes a lot of time. Training the neural net also takes time, so updating a neural net is not a trivial process. This is why most vendors that offer a neural net have limited refreshes on it. Setting up and administering a neural net is not a small undertaking and should be well thought out.

How Do I Use the Results?

- The neural net will typically provide a ranged score. In some cases it will provide a pass or fail answer. You will have to set up the system to interpret these results.

Building This In-House

One of the biggest questions you will have to ask yourself in building a neural net is whether you want to base their neural net and modeling off of good or bad behavior. I believe that you should use heuristics and rules-based checks for bad behavior and use neural nets for trying to predict good behavior.

If you look at a typical business you will find that the majority of orders that come in are good orders, not fraudulent. In modeling you need data, and lots of it, to build an effective predictive model. If a typical merchant did 100 orders and had a fraud rate of only 1%, would you rather build their model off of 1 order or 99 orders?

Furthermore, fraud is a moving target – new schemes and techniques are constantly being developed to get around these fraud techniques. If you base their modeling on bad behavior you are only going to catch the types of fraud you already know about. What about the schemes you have never heard of?

By focusing on good behavior I can look at an order and attempt to predict the answer for "How much does this order look like the other orders I have had that successfully processed without fraud?"

Data is king when it comes to modeling. If their volume is not very high, think about working with a group of other merchants in the same vertical space to share data and to help make even more predictive models.

Don't lose sight of the "insult" – You could build a solution that will catch all fraud attempts, but at what cost? How many good consumers will their solution peg as bad or risky consumers when the order is just fine? This is a major thing to consider as it can cost their business millions of dollars. In studies I have done on tools such as address verification, if you relied solely on AVS as the decision maker on risk you could "insult" up to 25% of your good consumers.

Chapter 33

Out-of-Pocket Checks

Out-of-wallet checks are intended to validate the consumer's identity by asking them questions that are derived from his past credit or public records. Most typically using credit reports. Typically includes five to ten questions in a multiple-choice format.

How Good Is It?

As a general tool, the out-of-wallet checks are very effective at establishing consumer identity. Although you have no guarantees using this service, you do have some good ammunition in fighting a charge-back. Only the most severe cases of identity theft would be able to pass this check.

The pros and cons of out-of-pocket checks are:

- Good tool for establishing consumer identity
- Best practice technique for credit issuance
- Does not translate well for international orders
- Does not require you to get a credit score

Considerations When Implementing or Buying This Functionality

- Can be costly to use.
- Requires a lot more intrusive information from a consumer, some may be very reluctant to give this much information unless they are buying something very expensive, or they are requesting credit.
- Does require that you integrate questions either directly into your web page checkout process, or the use of third-party pop-up verification screens.

- Typically requires SSN and/or date of birth. Some of the more recent services are using the last four of the SSN with DOB.

Estimated Costs - Typically this service is offered on a per-transaction basis. Because it requires the use of a credit report, costs tend to be significantly higher than using a fraud-screening service.

Alternative Solutions - Verified by Visa, MasterCard Securecode, reverse address and reverse phone number look up

Vendors - Experian, Lightbridge, ChoicePoint, Lexis-Nexis

How Does it Work?

Using the credit report the service will create questions based on the consumer's past spending history. For example:

What is the name of the bank/financial institution you financed your car with in 1997?
a) a) Chase Bank
b) Mitsubishi Motors Credit
c) Land Rover Credit
d) Ford Motor Credit

Typically there are five to ten questions with about a 50/50 split on recent versus past activity. Questions usually come from a variety of points such as car loans, home mortgages and credit cards.

How Do I Use the Results?

The consumer answers all of the questions and the service informs the merchant if the identity was verified (that is, whether they pass or fail). It is possible to utilize a service such as this without getting a credit score. If the consumer fails, you can route them to another channel to try and convert the order, or you can have them mail in payment.

If someone fails this process, make sure you only send correspondence, either mail or phone to the address and phone listed from the service you used. Don't send it to the address the new consumer used unless it happens to be a full match to the one on the service bureau record. This is important to ensure you are not aiding an identity theft perpetrator.

Building this in-house
N/A

Chapter 34

Reverse Look-ups: Phone & Address

The reverse lookup is used to cross check the address and phone information a consumer has provided to you with a third-party resource to verify that the public records show the same consumer's name is associated with the provided address and phone information.

How Good Is It?

Typically the reverse lookup is used in manual reviews to do one more verification of a consumer's address and phone information when AVS is not a full match. These checks can be somewhat suspect. Most of the services utilize public records for this information, and have to be updated with new information. This type of check can pull up a lot of false positives on fraud, if it is used in single pass-fail type of scenario. It does provide value in that when you can verify the information through public records and the shipping address is the same as on record, you have far less risk with the order.

"Gotchas" with reverse look-ups include:

- There are a lot of ways to fool this test
- There are people who move a lot, such as military families, in which multiple phone numbers and address may be in the public records
- There are lag periods between refreshes of the address and phone data
- In cases of identity theft, a fraudster can set up these services to look completely legitimate

- Good secondary test for checking AVS data when it is not a full match
- Typically cannot validate unlisted phone numbers
- More and more people are listing cell phone numbers and business phone numbers
- If you use it to check the shipping address, there are valid cases in which a consumer could be sending packages or gifts to a relative's home to pick up later

Considerations When Implementing or Buying This Functionality

- Available as a hosted bureau service or you can purchase monthly and quarterly SW distribution of data
- How often will your provider update the information or update their software?
- Will the data include cell phones and business phones?
- Are there any dead spots where information is not provided such as, international, Canada, Puerto Rico?
- What is the accuracy of the data they have? Try them out: Have ten people's information from around the country and see how well the service validates the information. Include someone who has been in place for a while, one that has recently moved and one that owns multiple properties.

Estimated Costs – Typically this service is offered on a per-transaction basis, but you can also purchase it as a subscription. There are some very low cost providers online, that have hosted screens for you to input data manually as well. This service is usually fairly inexpensive.

Alternative Solutions – Fraud-scoring solution that includes this capability, delivery address verification service that provides associated phone data with an address. Do geolocation validation on the zip code or area code.

Vendors – First Logic, Group One, Acxiom, InfoUSA

How does it Work?

If using it as a manual tool, you would enter the individual's address and phone information into a hosted screen or utility their IT shop has set up for you, and the service or application would come back with some mix of the following types of reverse look up results:

- I input the address and phone and it gave me the name of the person associated with each piece.
- I input the phone number only and it gives the address and name associated with it.
- I input an address and it gives me the phone and name associated with it.

How Do I Use the Results?

You verify this data and see if it matches. You can do this test on the billing and/or shipping address. But beware — there are a lot of valid reasons why the shipping address could be different. If however you got a full match on AVS, and you cannot validate the address contact the bank. If you got a full match on AVS but cannot match the phone information, contact the consumer for the correct information, or the bank if the number ends up being incorrect.

Building This In-House

Remember you need to make sure you ask the consumer for their home phone number and billing address.

Chapter 35

Return E-mail

Return e-mail is used to validate the consumer by sending them an e-mail at the time of purchase with a code, password or link they have to use to validate and complete the sale.

How Good Is It?

The return e-mail was primarily used to validate the consumer's e-mail address. This check is not really good for traditional retail or businesses that are looking to have a one-time real-time purchase process. This is better suited to businesses that are doing digital download or service-oriented businesses that will not physically ship goods to a consumer. In these cases the e-mail is the most important link with the consumer.

- Doesn't catch true identity theft cases.
- Slows down the checkout process.
- Very easy these days to set up e-mails in free domains.

Considerations When Implementing or Buying This Functionality

- Will you use passwords and codes or will you provide a link for the consumer to complete their sale?
- What will the impact be on your business if it takes 1-24 hours more to close a sale?
- How will this affect your order management and fulfillment processes?

Estimated Costs – Very low. You can easily set this up within your systems using your existing mail servers.

Alternative Solutions – Reverse address and phone number checks

Vendors – N/A

How does it Work?

It's a three-step process:

1. When a new consumer comes to do business you will need to collect their e-mail address and have them verify it before they close the screen. You will tell the consumer to expect an e-mail within a pre-set time frame that will provide them a password, link or code they will have to use on their site to complete their sale. When the consumer presses the buy button you will put the order into a holding status and you will send out an e-mail to the consumer.

2. When the consumer receives the e-mail, it will instruct them to use the provided link and to either input a code or password to validate the e-mail and the purchase.

3. You then provide them their service. For digital download providers this link could be to the point at which the consumer downloads the software.

How Do I Use the Results?

If you cannot get back to the consumer via the e-mail they provided, you should not send or allow them to download goods.

Building This In-House

Remember you should have good systems in place to check for consumers that are failing multiple times. Make sure you implement good hot lists and warm lists to prevent fraudsters from working your site to get in.

Put in velocity of use checks to see how many e-mails are associated with a consumer's data points such as, address, phone number and credit card number.

Credit Card Fraud

Chapter 36

Rules Engines

The rules engine is a middleware application that allows the creation and prioritization of rules to be used in managing fraud. These engines allow merchants to create rules that will be evaluated on orders as they come in. The rules engine can have many different names, such as "decisioning software," "management software" or "order management." Most payment, CRM, and order management systems will have some of the capabilities to build and apply rules.

How Good Is It?

You can use a rules engine to help you prevent fraud. The rules engine gives you the ability to perform pre- and post-authorization tests and rules, so you can have logic on how and when you want to call for an authorization and you can have rules to handle the return results from authorization.

Merchants having been applying rules to their order flow for years. The concept of a rules engine does not derive from the growth of fraud, merchants have had to build rules to process the order. For example, merchants need rules to add tax based on the consumer's location and to add shipping based on their preference. With fraud, merchants have reacted to losses by having their IT Departments add rules to their order management system to weed out orders they may not want to take or to separate orders that they may want to manually review (e.g., all orders over a certain dollar amount).

The intent of the rules engine is to provide the business owner with a way to add new rules to their order process to look for fraud. Good rules engines allow technical novices to apply their fraud expertise to add very complex rules that can automate the review of orders without manual intervention.

Good rules engines also provide a mechanism to more quickly make changes to the order flow if you are getting burned by fraud. This is crucial to being successful at minimizing the impact of a fraud ring. Think about it, if your company was being hit by a fraud ring, and you can see the characteristics to look for, and you are in their peak holiday season, how long would it take to get your IT Department to implement a new rule to prevent these orders from processing? Could they even do it without bringing down the business for a time period? In reality I have seen that this can take as long as a month to implement a new rule without a rules engine in place.

Rules engines also:

- Put the control of the fraud-prevention process back into the hands of the fraud-prevention owner.
- Allow you to more quickly react to new fraud schemes, by applying new rules in real time.
- Allow you to automate the separation of orders more quickly and efficiently, reducing the number of orders to manually review
- Give you better insight to the processes that are in place.
- Have a high cost to get started.
- Require someone to manage the fraud business processes.
- Add additional software and hardware burden to ongoing costs.

Considerations When Implementing or Buying This Functionality

- How does the solution integrate into your current business flow?
- Do you have to have a technical background to operate the solution?
- Could anyone looking at your business process in the rules engine understand it? Or do you have to learn how to interpret it?
- How fast can you add or change a rule?
- Does the engine manage only a list of rules or does it allow you to set up a business process flow?
- Does the solution integrate other fraud-prevention techniques such as geolocation, velocity and/or hot lists?
- What type of graphical user interface does the solution come with?
- Do you just get back a pass, fail or review or do you get the results of all of the tests?

Estimated Costs - Moderate, you will typically pay for a software purchase. There are a couple of providers that offer all of these services on a hosted and managed basis.

Alternative Solutions - Fraud Scoring

Vendors - CyberSource, Fair Isaac, Retail Decisions, Clear Commerce

How Does it Work?

The rule engine concept is pretty simple to understand. You write some rules and the engine will run those rules against an order when it is submitted. But in actuality there are a couple of ways this can be done, and you need to make sure you understand that the solution you are looking at is going to do what you really want it to do.

Type 1 - The rules engine allows you to add rules into a list of checks and then when an order is processed against the engine, it will evaluate the rules one at a time. The first rule to fail, fails the entire transaction. No other rules beyond the first failed rule will be run. This type typically will not allow for very complicated comparisons.

This type of rules engine is simple to set up and maintain, and produces a pass or fail type of answer. One of the major shortfalls of this solution is that not all of the rules are run, so if you try to look at a failed order, you will only see the first rule that failed, making it more difficult to determine which orders you should spend more time trying to convert. This type also is hard to interpret what is actually being checked. So if you have high turnover of staff, this solution can be a little more difficult to understand for staff coming in.

Type 2 - The rules engine allows you to add rules into a list of checks and apply weights to each of the rules to allow for some rules to be treated as more risky than others. When an order is processed against this type of rules engine, all of the rules are run, and weights are applied to each and the rules engine then creates a score that will determine the outcome of the order. This type can support pass, fail or review outcomes. This type is the hardest to interpret what is actually being checked. So if you have high turnover of staff, this solution can be a little more difficult to understand for staff coming in.

This type of rules engine is a little more complex to set up. You will have to understand how to weight certain conditions in order to get the effective results from the solution. It will require more intensive management.

Type 3 – The rules engine allows you to add rules into a business flow, indicating which outcomes or rules need to be run based on the outcome of any one particular rule. When an order is processed through this solution, the number of actual rules run against the order could be different for every order processed because the number of rules run is based on the outcomes of each rule and the order's data points. This type can produce a pass, fail or review response.

This type of rules engine is little more complex to set up, but offers a much easier way to view and describe the business flow. This type offers the greatest flexibility for adding or changing the rule logic, by allowing you to blend the rules for fraud prevention with the business processes you use to make a decision on an order.

Type 4 – The rules engine is designed to be an all-encompassing engine that provides a merchant with the ability to set up and manage all of the fraud-prevention tools under one application. This gives the merchant the capability to write and edit rules and integrate new prevention tools more rapidly and effectively. With this type of rules engine, you can alter your risk-prevention capabilities on the back-end without having to touch the code in your front-end systems each time you need to make a change.

The rules engine evaluates orders using a previously deployed strategy. This part of the rules engine provides a way to encompass other business processes and fraud techniques into the solution, such as payment processing, fraud scoring, geolocation, credit checks and age verification.

Inside the rules engine you will have the ability to set up business strategies that represent your risk management decisions and consist of workflows and rules. The workflows represent a collection of rules and a rule compares data points of a transaction to a set of conditions, or it can compare data points to other data points. Think of them as IF/THEN statements that you are writing and that express what elements you look at for predicting risk.

How Do I Use the Results?

Rules engines are great at automating the fraud-prevention business process. Make sure you take this into account when you are deciding the outcomes you want from the solution. Try to maximize the number of orders going into the accept and reject buckets, while minimizing the number of orders you want to review.

Make sure their calling applications don't contain any rules or logic. If you set them up to look for the pass, fail or review, you free yourself up to add and manipulate rules in their rules engine and not in their production system.

Building This In-House

N/A

Chapter 37

Secure Tokens

Secure tokens use a device to create a unique number to authenticate the end user. Typically these devices have been used in network security, but there are vendors now offering this type of solution for consumer authentication.

How Good Is It?

The device is a good way to ensure that the consumer is who they say they are. To use this solution you have to have the consumer and merchant participating for it to work. It requires the consumer carry a "fob" to produce the unique number. And it requires the merchant to have the ability to authenticate the number the "fob" created. It is not likely that a fraudster will be able to mimic or copy the number, as they change every minute, but the device can be stolen by a fraudster.

Typically this solution is offered by a particular merchant or bank and the consumers can use it at any of the participating merchant locations. If they go outside of the supported merchant base the tool is useless, and the regular fraud-prevention techniques come into play. Market adoption of this type of solution is extremely low.

Secure tokens as a fraud-prevention technique:

- Doesn't catch true identity theft cases.
- Requires the consumer carry a "fob."
- Requires all merchants to support the validation of the number.
- Is a good method to get non-traditional e-commerce or MOTO customers to make purchases through these channels.

Considerations When Implementing or Buying This Functionality

- What type of device or "fob" does the solution offer?
- Will the device work with any other merchant site?
- Who provides customer support if the "fob" is defective?
- How long is the "fob" going to last?
- Does the device use a unique PIN combined with the Fob to increase the security?

Estimated Costs - Moderate

Alternative Solutions - Smart cards, consumer authentication

Vendors - Cardinal Commerce, RSA

How Does it Work?

The merchant or bank issues the consumer a "fob." This is a device the size of a key that creates a unique number every minute. These fobs come in different sizes and shapes, and you can get them as key rings or credit cards. The consumer is also issued a PIN to use with the unique number.

When the consumer is ready to make a purchase, he or she goes to a merchant that supports the technology and they chose what they want to buy and then start the check-out process. When going through the buy process, the consumer will be asked to give the PIN and the unique number generated by the fob. The merchant will likely be going to a third-party service that has an application that can match the exact number the fob will create to see if the number provided by the consumer matches or not. If it does you have authenticated the consumer, if it does not you would then reject the order or attempt another authentication technique.

How Do I Use the Results?

If the consumer can authenticate via the secure token, then you would accept the order. If the consumer cannot authenticate, you would reject the order. If a consumer comes in that is not using the secure token, you will have to have processes in place to catch fraud with these orders.

If you support this type of solution you should also set up a process to confirm a card is not supposed to be using a secure token. This will prevent you from processing an order for a consumer that had their card stolen, and is being used fraudulently.

Building This In-House

N/A

Chapter 38

Smart Cards

Smart cards have implanted chips that can be read by specialized devices to authenticate that the card is authentic. They don't authenticate the consumer, they authenticate the card is real. Some implementations called "chip and PIN" actually use the combination of a chip to authenticate the card and require consumers to enter a PIN to authenticate themselves.

How Good Is It?

Smart cards are a great concept, and they are pretty reliable when it comes to fraud prevention. Currently there are sporadic card issuers with smart cards, such as the American Express Blue Card. But for the most part adoption is still very low.

The biggest downside of the smart card is the required reader to check the chip. Until the time comes that a chip reader can be put on all computers, phones and terminals this technology will be slow to be adopted. To the consumer, there really is no incentive to use this technology unless they are simply "scared" of having the card or number stolen.

The fact is most merchants are not set up to handle these cards either, and they are simply using these as normal credit cards in their process, thereby stripping any fraud-prevention value the technique may have offered.

Smart cards:
- Are good for preventing counterfeit cards
- Rely on physical card reader to work the secure check
- Work like a normal card when no reader is available
- Are not highly adopted today

- Are part of major initiatives in Europe to switch to this technology

Considerations When Implementing or Buying This Functionality
- Make sure their processor supports the services
- Make sure you can get card readers to their consumer

Estimated Costs – Low to high

Alternative Solutions – Consumer authentication

Vendors – Visa, MasterCard, American Express, Discover

How Does it Work?

The issuing bank issues a branded credit card that has an embedded chip that is unique. When a consumer makes a purchase in which the merchant has a specialized reader that can read the chip, the chip and mag strip data is checked when the card is swiped.

Readers are available for card-present transactions and for computers. Some issuers actually send out a card reader to the consumer with the card. The basic use of the card is the same as a standard credit card; the chip is just a means to make sure the card is authentic.

How Do I Use the Results?

If the consumer can authenticate via the smart card, then you would accept the order. If the consumer cannot authenticate, you would reject the order. If a consumer comes in that is not using the reader you will have to have processes in place to catch fraud with these orders.

If you support this type of solution you should also set up a process to confirm a card is not supposed to be using a reader. This will prevent you from processing an order for a consumer that had their card stolen, and is being used fraudulently.

Building This In-House

N/A

Chapter 39

Velocity of Use

The intent of velocity of use is to look for suspicious behavior based on the number of associated transactions a consumer is attempting. It works based on counting the number of uses of a data element within a predetermined timeframe. The theory is the higher the number of uses on a data element (e.g., credit cards) in a predefined time period (e.g., 24 hours), the higher the risk of taking an order.

For example:

How many times has credit number "111111111111111" been used in the last 24 hours?

How Good Is It?

Velocity of use is a building block of any serious fraud-prevention solution. Keeping track of the number of uses by different data elements allows you to spot unusual trends and it allows you spot run-up activity. Most major fraud-screening solutions have this type of functionality built into it.

- Velocity of use is good for detecting fraud rings, multiple fraud attacks from the same perpetrator and also can catch some forms of identity morphing.
- The more data elements you can track velocity of use on, the more effective the tool is. Good data elements to perform this test on are: credit card number, address, phone number, e-mail address and account number.

- If you establish accounts for your customers, perform velocity of use on the number of accounts associated with a particular individual.

Considerations When Implementing or Buying This Functionality

- Decide up front on the data elements you want to perform velocity of use checks on. You will also need to know the number of uses you want to flag and the time interval you want look in.
- You will have to perform some normalization on the addresses if you are doing this in-house to ensure you get matches.
- Make sure you are logging usage for all attempts, not just completed or valid orders.
- Plan on maintaining data for at least 12 months. I recommend 18 months.
- Will you want to have a pass/fail velocity of use check or a graduated scale type of solution? The graduated scale adds more risk as the number of uses increases. So a set of 3 orders happening in 5 minutes would have more risk than a set of 3 orders happening over 30 days.
- There is a distinct advantage to using a third-party service that combines data from multiple merchants or banks to track velocity of use, as you get a much fuller picture on activity by a potential fraudster, and have a better chance at picking up on run-up activity.

Estimated Costs – Costs to implement a simple velocity of use tool are low, as long as you already have database resources you can utilize, and the applications you use to process orders are easily integrated into. A lot of ERP, application servers, decision servers and the like on the market have this technology integrated into them.

Alternative Solutions – Fraud-Screening services have velocity of use already built in. Be sure to check if you can add your own custom fields. If you are looking at doing this check based on their account numbers you will have to look at purchasing in-house solutions or building this service on your own.

Look at velocity of change as well, as these two forms of velocity complement each other.

Vendors – CyberSource, Clear Commerce, Retail Decisions, HNC/Fair Isaac

How Does it Work?
The velocity of use technique requires a supporting database and two calls to work. One call increases the count on a data element while the second call does a look up to see what the count is. If you are using a commercial solution or you are getting this functionality from a commercial fraud-screening service, you will only see one call to acquire this information as the solution will hide these calls from you

Based on the look up call you will get a pass or fail type of response and you will have to decide to reject, review or pass the order to another sales channel, such as telephone order.

There are three components to performing a velocity of use check: the data element, the count and the time interval.

Typically the data elements used for velocity of use are the address (address, state, zip code), phone number, credit card number and e-mail address. Name is not recommended as there are to many people with similar names and this could really kill their sales or fill their manual review bins. The address has to be looked at in whole, not in parts, counting the number by state or zip code can raise a lot of false alarms. If you typically don't do a lot of business in one location in a short timeframe you may want to look at zip code or state. Likewise if you have identified a hot spot by zip code, you should apply a rule to perform further fraud-prevention tests on that order.

The count and timeframe are very tightly joined. There is no hard, set rule on what number of changes and timeframe to look at. In general you need to understand your good customers, know if you get a lot of repeat business, know if is it typical for your customers to make more than one purchase per day, week or year? You also need to think about when it becomes completely unrealistic.

Examples:
1. I sell printer ink, paper and refills – I would expect my customers to be repeat customers, and I would assume on non-b2b orders that consumers would not typically make more than one purchase per day, but it would not be unusual for a consumer to do two orders in one day, but three or more orders in one day would be highly suspect.
2. I sell laptop computers – I would expect my b2c customers to have more one time purchases with at least 12 months time between

orders. I would be suspect of any b2c customer making more than one order per day on computers. This does not mean ordering more than one computer in an order, this means placing two separate orders for computers in one day or week.

3. I sell jewelry – I would expect my b2c customers to only make one purchase a day, and would be very suspect of two or more orders in a day. I would be somewhat suspect of more than one order in a week or month, and would want to take a closer look, and I routinely have b2c customers that make more than one purchase in a year.

4. I sell rechargeable cell phones – I would be highly suspect of more than one recharge in a day, I would be slightly suspect of more than one recharge in a week, and expect a recharge every other week or once a month.

The better commercial solutions, usually fraud-screening services, don't simply pass and fail on velocity of use. They actually increment the level of risk by the number of uses until they reach a point that they reject the order. This is usually only found in solutions that allow weighting of tests. For example: If I am looking at a time interval of 15 minutes and a credit card number with only one use comes up I would get no added risk, but if the same credit card showed up twice in 5 minutes I would give it high risk. The more attempts in the time period, the higher the risk goes. Likewise the more time that passes between attempts, the lower the risk.

Set up a process that mandates that all attempted orders are logged into velocity, not just valid sales.

How Do I Use the Results?

- Log all attempted transactions, not just valid orders coming into the system.
- You can set up their velocity of use tests to look for orders to review or reject, but if you are going to reject based on velocity of use, make sure they fail other fraud tests as well. If the only test they fail is velocity of use, we would recommend you call the customer to validate the purchases.
- 90 days is the magic number before charge-backs appear, which means they won't appear on a hot list until up to 90 days. Some fraudsters will time their attacks so orders are coming in at odd intervals: one order today, next one in three days, the next in one

week, the next in four days etc. Make sure some of your velocity of use tests are looking at activity within the 90-day window. You can do this real time or to save processing time in the upfront orders, set up an off-line batch routine that looks at activity by accounts or orders to establish counts over the 90-day window.

- If someone fails this test and you are looking at a time period less than 24 hours, MAKE SURE YOU CANCEL OR PUT ON HOLD the original orders.

Building This In-House

The velocity of use technique requires a supporting database and two calls to work. One call increases the count on a data element while the second call does a look up to see what the count is.

Database – Have your Database Administrator set up a database resource for you to use. They will have to set up the database structure and design to store the data elements, and to maintain counts on the data elements.

Call One: Add Records and Increment – Have your IT team set up calls from all applications and channels that touch those data elements, so e-commerce, MOTO and card-present channels will add new entries into the data set or they will increment the counts on the data elements if they already exist. You have to enter a date time stamp with every new record you put into the data set.

Call Two: Look Up Activity – Have your IT team set up call from all applications and channels that touch these data elements, typically done as part of your fraud-screening procedures, to check the number of uses this person has. This is typically done by use of stored procedure or in the event you are using only one record per data element and are incrementing the count and date time stamp you would only have to call the supporting data set and look up the data element. This call is doing the look up on each independent data element you have determined to do velocity of use checks on.

Chapter 40

Velocity of Change

The intent of velocity of change is to look for suspicious behavior based on the number of changes between data elements on new transactions with previous transactions. It works based on counting the number of changes with associated data elements within a predefined timeframe. The theory is the higher the number of changes on a set of data elements, such as the number of phone numbers or addresses associated with credit cards in a predefined timeframe, the higher the risk of taking an order.

For example:

How many phone numbers have been used with credit card number "111111111111111" in the last 24 hours?

How Good Is It?

Velocity of change is one of the mechanisms to catch identity morphing. As a general fraud-prevention tool, there is a high correlation to risky behavior with those transactions that fail this type of test. Most major fraud-screening solutions have this type of functionality built into it.

- Velocity of change is good for detecting stolen card numbers, multiple fraud attacks from the same perpetrator, and also for detecting some forms of identity morphing.
- The more data elements you can track velocity of change on the more effective the tool is. Good data elements to perform this test on are: credit card numbers, addresses (billing and shipping), phone number, e-mail address and account number.

184

- If you establish accounts for your customers performing velocity of change on the number of accounts associated with a particular individual data element or in the opening of new accounts can help catch fraudsters before they can place a fraudulent order.

Considerations When Implementing or Buying This Functionality

- Decide up front on the data elements you want to perform velocity of change checks on. You will also need to know the number of changes you want to flag and the time interval you want to look in.
- You will have to perform some normalization on the addresses if you are doing this in-house to ensure you get matches.
- Use the shipping address, and not the billing address, for their velocity of change. See guidelines and samples under How it Works.
- Make sure you are logging usage for all attempts, not just completed or valid orders.
- Plan on maintaining data for at least 12 months. I recommend 18 months.
- Will you want to have a pass/fail velocity of change check or a graduated scale type of solution? The graduated scale adds more risk as the number of changes increases. Typically with velocity of change the pass/fail method is used.
- There is a distinct advantage to using a third-party service that combines data from multiple merchants or banks to track velocity of change, as you get a much fuller picture on activity by a potential fraudster, and have a better chance at picking up on bust-out activity.

Estimated Costs - Costs to implement a simple velocity of change tool are low, as long as you already have database resources you can utilize, and the applications you use to process orders are easily integrated into. A lot of ERP, application servers, decision servers and the like on the market have this technology integrated into them already or through third-party modules.

Alternative Solutions - Fraud-screening services have velocity of change already built in. Be sure to check if you can add your own custom fields. If you are looking at doing this check based on account numbers you will have to look at purchasing in-house solutions or building this service on your own.

Vendors – CyberSource, Clear Commerce, Retail Decisions, HNC/Fair Isaac, Trustmarque

How Does it Work?
The velocity of change technique requires a supporting database and two calls to work. One call increases the count on a data element while the second call does a look up to see what the count is. If you are using a commercial solution or you are getting this functionality from a commercial fraud-screening service, you will only see one call to acquire this information as the solution will hide these calls from you.

Based on the look-up call you will get a pass or fail type of response and you will have to decide to reject, review or pass the order to another sales channel, such as telephone order.

There are four components to performing a velocity of change check, two data elements to compare, the count and the time interval.

Typically the data elements used for velocity of change are the shipping address (address, state, zip code), phone number, credit card number, expiration date and e-mail address. Name is not recommended as there are too many people with similar names and this could really kill their sales or fill their manual review bins. The address has to looked at in whole not in parts, counting the number by state or zip code can raise a lot of false alarms. If you typically don't do a lot of business in one location in a short timeframe you may want to look at zip code or state. Likewise if you have identified a hot spot by zip code, you should be applying a rule to perform further fraud-prevention tests on that order by looking at changes within that zip code.

The count and time frame are very tightly joined. There is no hard, set rule on what number of changes and timeframe to look at. In general you need to understand your good customers: Do you get a lot of repeat business? Is it typical for your customers to make more than one purchase per day, week or year? You also need to think about when it becomes completely unrealistic.
In order to see change, you have to be comparing two data elements to count the number of times one piece of the information changes. This forms the basis of the technique.

Examples:

My customers are typically buying my products or services as gifts for other people.

1. **Credit card number to expiration date** – Checking to see how many times the expiration date changes with the credit card number
2. **Credit card number to shipping address** – Checking to see how many shipping addresses are associated with a credit card number
3. **Credit card number to phone number** – Checking to see how many phone numbers have been given with a credit card number
4. **Credit card number to e-mail** – Checking to see how many e-mails are given with credit card number
5. **Phone number to shipping address** – Checking to see how many shipping addresses are given with phone number
6. **Phone number to credit card** – Checking to see how many credit cards are given with a phone number
7. **Phone number to e-mail** – Checking to see how many e-mails are given with phone number
8. **Shipping address to credit card number** – Checking to see how many credit card numbers are associated with a shipping address

The better commercial solutions, usually fraud-screening services, perform these velocity of change tests.

Set up a process that mandates that all attempted orders are logged into velocity, not just valid sales.

How Do I Use the Results?

- Log all attempted transactions, not just valid orders coming into the system
- You can set up your velocity of change tests to look for orders to review or reject
- 90 days is the magic number before charge-backs appear, which means they won't appear on a hot list until up to 90 days. Some fraudsters will time their attacks so orders are coming in at odd intervals: one order today, next one in three days, the next in one week, the next in four days etc. Make sure some of your velocity of change tests are looking at activity within the 90-day window. You can do this real time, or to save processing time in the upfront orders set up an offline batch routine that looks at activity by accounts or orders to establish counts over the 24-hour window by under the 90-day window. For orders that are over 90 days old, and

have not been charged back, you don't need to perform active checks.

- If someone fails this test and you are looking at a time period less than 24 hours, MAKE SURE YOU CANCEL OR PUT ON HOLD any other orders from this identity.
- The following are meant as starting points only, you have to look at their customer base to determine what time intervals and number of changes really are best for you.
    - **Credit card number to expiration date** – More than 2 changes in 24 hours, they could make one typo, but to see three changes indicates guessing.
    - **Credit card number to shipping address** – If your products are normally sent as gifts, you should set this high, if you use it at all. This is really better for businesses that don't normally have consumers buying gifts.
    - **Credit card number to phone number** – More than 2 changes in 24 hours shows guessing and high usage and is considered risky.
    - **Credit card number to e-mail** –Most consumers online use the same e-mail address for making purchases. If you start to see multiple e-mail addresses more than two, you should do further review.
    - **Phone number to shipping address** – Again if you do a lot of gifts, you should not use this test, as you will get a lot of changes with this indicator. Usually a good indicator of bogus phone numbers
    - **Phone number to credit card** – Most online consumers use one to three credit cards for online purchase. If you see more than four associated with a phone number you need to review or reject the order.
    - **Phone number to e-mail** – Again more than two changes and you need to do some other checks.
    - **Shipping address to credit card number** – Typical online consumers use between one and three credit cards for purchasing online, so look for more than four changes.

Building This In-House

The velocity of change technique requires a supporting database and two calls to work. One call increases the count on a data element test while the second call does a look-up to see what the count is.

Database – Have your Database Administrator set up a database resource for you to use. They will have to set up the database structure and design to store the data elements, and to maintain counts on the data elements as changes are documented.

Call One: Add Records and Increment – Have your IT team set up calls from all applications and channels that touch those data elements, so e-commerce, MOTO and card-present channels will add new entries into the data set or they will increment the counts on the data elements if they already exist. You have to enter a date time stamp with every new record you put into the data set.

Call Two: Look Up Activity – Have your IT team set up call from all applications and channels that touch these data elements, typically done as part of their fraud-screening procedures, to check the number of changes this order has. This is typically done by use of stored procedure or in the event you are using only one record per data element and are incrementing the count and date time stamp you would only have to call the supporting data set and look up the data element. This call is doing the look up on each independent data element you have determined to do velocity of change checks on.

Chapter 41

Verified by Visa

Verified by Visa is an emerging tool that is intended to validate that the authorized credit card holder is the one actually attempting to make a purchase.

How Good Is It?

In general the concept of authenticating the consumer is a good one. For the merchant, this is an excellent tool since it is one of the first tools that actually offers some financial coverage if fraud does occur. The card associations implemented these programs to increase consumer confidence in making purchases online, and to help protect online merchants from fraud.

The main reason you want to implement this service is the protection it offers from fraud-related charge-backs. Not everything is protected, so make sure you review the details of the program with Visa and MasterCard. There are significant differences on what is covered in the U.S. versus what is covered in Europe. Some examples of what is not covered by the program include: purchases made with procurement cards, recurring billing, split shipments or back-ordered goods, "one-click" technology sales, transactions in which the consumer cannot be authenticated. It also seems that certain high-risk segments, such as adult and gaming, are not going to be covered. So if you are in these vertical markets you should check before you buy. There is no threshold set for risk, but there is wording that suggests a threshold for fraud rates will be set and you will have to keep your losses below that. Also you have to properly set the e-commerce-preferred indicator.

The other major benefit of the Verified by Visa tool is the simplification of some of their charge-back resolution activities. For those orders in which the consumer was participating in the program and you did authenticate them, the resolution process would occur between the issuing bank and the consumer, not between you and the consumer.

Consumers may be legitimate even if they can't authenticate. Some examples of reasons why good customers may not be able to authenticate include: The use of software the prevents pop-up windows will render this service obsolete, the pop-up can time out or consumers that were pre-registered may not know they have a password or PIN to use this.

Considerations When Implementing or Buying This Functionality

- The current consumer authentication tools offered by Visa are meant for and work only on e-commerce transactions. You have to have fraud processes to handle your MOTO traffic.
- For these programs to work the merchant, consumer, issuer and acquiring bank must all be participating in the program. So make sure your acquiring bank is set up to support the e-commerce indicator, and check on their certification requirements.
- For European merchants, some of the acquiring banks are still not set up to support consumer authentication.
- You still need to perform other fraud checks. This tool does not cover many of the card types on the market today. There are legitimate cases in which you may not be able to complete the authentication process with the consumer and you still need to make sure their overall fraud rates are kept within standards. Also the industry expects some fraud shift to cards not offering this service.
- Companies doing little transactional volume should consider using a outserviced service bureau to perform this service.
- Make sure you are checking and providing all of the correct data points: You have to not it as e-commerce with the ECI, and you must check the AVS, you must check for enrollment, you need the CAVV/AVV, shows the order was checked for enrollment and you need the XID the unique transaction number.
- You will have to get a digital certificate from Visa, which takes about two weeks. See your acquiring bank to get the form.

Estimated Costs – You can find this service available as an outsourced service, or as a software application that you can implement in-house. The actual cost to purchase the software is fairly low – a couple of thousand dollars to purchase. You will have to pay annual maintenance on the software. You will have to make changes to your front-end e-commerce engine.

Alternative Solutions – None

Vendors – Arcot, CyberSource, Clear Commerce. CyberSource uses Arcot as their underlying technology and are the only ones offering a transaction-based model to implement consumer authentication.

How Does it Work?

The process used by the consumer authentication services to authenticate consumers is pretty simple. The consumer enrolls with the issuing bank and is given a password, PIN or device to authenticate himself or herself. When the consumer makes a purchase online the consumer is asked to give that password, PIN or device to authenticate.

The purchase sequence can be broken down into five stages, first the consumer goes through the checkout procedure the same way they do today providing the same data fields they do today. When the buy button is pressed the consumer's system, using the commercially available software on the market, sends a message to Visa to find out if the consumer is participating in the consumer authentication program. If the cardholder is participating in the program, the card association service will send a pop-up window to the consumer. The pop-up looks as if it is coming from the issuing bank of the consumer, asking them to enter their password or PIN. The bank then validates this password or PIN and returns the results to the merchant.

For these programs to work the merchant, consumer, issuer and acquiring bank must all be participating in the program. Consumer adoption is slow at best. According to Visa, about 10 million cardholders are enrolled as of October 2002. Likewise merchant adoption has been slow. Merchant enrollment should increase in the U.S. since in April 2003 the financial coverage for certain orders took effect.

Consumers are being enrolled by self-registration, issuer auto enrollment and issuer prompted registration.

The liability shift is different based on the region you are doing business in and the type of charge-back you have. For the Visa program you will be covered from charge-backs that are coded as RC23, RC61 and RC75. For the Visa program you only have to check to see if they are enrolled to get coverage. Remember though if they are enrolled and they can't authenticate you get no liability shift. Currently for European transactions, in which the cardholder and merchant are European, you have the liability shift already for both card types. For the U.S. the liability shift for Visa started in April 2003.

From a security perspective, all communication between the consumer and issuing bank is secured, you as a merchant will not see or ask for this password. The pop-up window the end user receives contains a secret message that only the consumer knows that shows the consumer that the pop-up window is real and not a fake that someone made to try and steal the password.

There has been a fraud case in which fraudsters acquired account information and then called the issuing bank and changed the address information and signed up for Verified by Visa. The fraudsters then made a lot of fraudulent transactions. The merchants will be covered as long as they followed the rules.

1. "Visa Starts Password Service to fight Online Fraud," By Saul Hansell, The New York Times on the Web, www.nytimes.com. Published on December 3, 2001
Dell Computer (news/quote), by contrast, signed on to be among the first merchants to participate in the Verified by Visa program, but mainly to reduce the number of people who call to order computers because they are afraid to enter their card numbers on the web.

"We're not greatly concerned about fraud levels," said Sam Decker, Dell's senior manager for consumer e-business. "We want to give customers more confidence in buying online."

Moreover, in 2003, Visa expects to change these rules so that merchants that accept Verified by Visa will not be liable for unauthorized charges. That promise is not enough to get Amazon.com, the largest online store, to participate in Verified by Visa.

"From our standpoint, the amount of friction that Verified by Visa introduces for the customer outweighs the benefit from reducing fraud," said Mark Britto, Amazon's director of corporate development. "It would turn one-click ordering into four-point, three-click ordering," he said, referring to the online store's trademark method of fast checkout.

How Do I Use the Results?

For Visa orders when you are using this technology you should implement the following:
- For orders in which the consumer is participating in the program, and the order type is a covered type, and the consumer successfully authenticates, accept the order.
- For orders in which the consumer is not participating in the program, and the order type is a covered type, you have checked for enrollment, and the order characteristics are within their normal order tolerances, accept the order.
- For orders in which the consumer is not participating in the program, and the order type is a covered type, you have checked for enrollment, and the order characteristics are not in-line with their normal orders, review the order or perform further fraud checks favoring sales conversion.
- For orders in which the consumer is participating in the program, and cannot successfully authenticate, and the order characteristics are in-line with their normal orders perform other fraud-screening checks or manually review the order favoring risk aversion.
- For non-Visa orders, perform traditional checks.

Building This In-House

N/A

Conclusion

What's Next?

In this book you have gained the knowledge you need to understand the framework and building blocks to effectively combat card-not-present credit card fraud. It is a lot of information to absorb, but there is more you need to do.

There was so much information that needed to be conveyed I could not do justice to discussing building an effective fraud-prevention strategy in one book. It would take another complete book to discuss the theories and methods that can be used to do this. You have the fundamentals now to understand the components of a fraud-prevention strategy, the techniques available to you to implement that strategy and a sample strategy and vendor listing to begin the process of developing your own strategy.

If this is your first introduction to controlling fraud, I hope this has put the bigger picture in perspective. If there are points in this book you want to discuss or you have seen other interesting techniques that can be of value to other merchants, send me an e-mail at davidamontague@fraudpractice.com.

Appendix A

Vendor Listing

This listing was created at the time of publishing, so some companies may have moved, closed or been purchased by other companies. Check the Internet for any updates or changes.

Likewise the services referenced in this book were available at the time of publishing, and some companies may have made changes to their offerings providing more or less services.

Seisint, Accurint, *Geolocation*
6601 Park of Commerce blvd
Boca Raton, FL 33487
561.999.4400
www.accurant.com

ACXIOM, *Reverse Lookups*
1 Information Way
Little Rock, AR 72202
888.322.9466
www.acxiom.com

Akamai, *Geolocation*
8 Cambridge Center
Cambridge, MA 02142
877.425.2624
www.akamai.com

Amazon.co.uk, *Age Verification, Adult verification Service*

Slough, Berkshire United Kingdom
www.avs.co.uk

American Express, *AAV+, Auth, CID*
200 Vesey Street
New York, NY 10285
212.640.2000
www.americanexpress.com

Arcot Systems, Inc, *Verified By Visa, Payer Authorization*
3200 Patrick Henry Drive
Santa Clara, CA 95054
www.arcot.com

Aristotle Inc, *Age Verification, Identity Verification*
205 Pennsylvania Avenue, SE
Washington, DC 2003
202.543.8345
www.aristotle.com
www.verifymyidentification.com

BioLink Technologies Inc., *Biometric*
Miramar, FL
800.611.1555
www.biolinkusa.com

Choicepoint, *Out-of-Pocket Checks, Fraud Scoring*
1000 Alderman Drive
Alpharetta, GA 3005
877.317.5000
www.choicepoint.com

Clear Commerce, *Decision Engine, Verified by Visa*
11921 North MoPac Expressway, Suite 400
Austin, TX 78749
512.832.0132
www.clearcommerce.com

CyberSource Corporation, *Fraud Screening, Consumer Authentication*
Mountain View, CA

650.965.6000
www.cybersource.com

Digital Envoy, *Geolocation*
250 Scientific Drive
Suite 800
Norcross, GA 30092
www.digitalenvoy.com

Dunn & Bradstreet, *Credit Checks for Businesses*
103 JFK Parkway
Short Hills, NJ 07078
973.921.5500
www.dnb.com

EFTDirect , *Charge-back Insurance*
3601 Partridge Path Suite 5
Ann Arbor, MI 48108
734.477.7700
www.eft-direct.com

Equifax, *Credit Reports, Fraud Scoring*
P.O Box 105873
Atlanta, GA 30348
888.202.4025
www.equifax.com

Ethentica Inc., *Biometric*
Aliso Viejo, CA
949.389.1850
www.ethentica.com

Euprise Inc., Infohood America, *Reverse Lookup*
34 Buckingham Palace Rd
Suite 170
Belgravia, London SW1WORH
UK
www.infohood.com
www.phonebusters.com

FraudScrub Inc, *Fraud Scoring, Consumer Authentication*
5555 Hollywood Blvd
Hollywood, FL 33021
954.987.5677
www.fraudscrub.com

Group One, *Delivery Address Verification*
4200 Parliament Place, Ste 600
Lanham, MD 20706-1844
888.413.6763
www.g1.com

Fair Isaac Corporation / HNC, *Fraud Screening, Decision Engine*
200 Smith Ranch Road
San Rafael, CA 94903
800.213.5542
www.fairisaac.com

Indentix Inc., *Biometric*
Sunnyvale, CA
408.731.2000
www.identix.com

Intelligent Search Technology Ltd., *Reverse Lookups DPC*
20 Milltown Road, Suite 202
Brewster, NY 10509
800.287.0412
www.name-searching.com

InfoSpace, *Reverse Lookups*
601 108th Avenue NE, Suite 1200
Bellevue, WA 98004
425.201.6100
www.infospace.com

InfoUSA, *Reverse lookups*
5711 S. 86th Circle
PO Box 27347
Omaha, NE 68127-0347
www.infousa.com

Jay Computer, *Zip Code & Area Code Lookup Services, Software*
9594 208th Street West
Lakeville, MN 55044
866.527.6266
www.nt.jcsm.com

Lexis-Nexis Group, *Fraud Scoring, Decision Engine, Suspect Address, Consumer Authentication*
P.O. Box 933
Dayton, Ohio 45401-0933
937.865.6800
www.lexisnexis.com

LightBridge, *Fraud Scoring, Credit Check, Out-of-Wallet Checks*
67 South Bedford Street
Burlington, MA 01803
781.359.4000

Margo Systems, *Fraud Scoring*
220 W. Huron Street, Suite 5000
Chicago, IL 60610
312.397.8880
www.margo.com

MasterCard International, *Consumer authentication, MasterCard SecureCode, Authorization, Address Verification Services, Card Security CVC2*
2000 Purchase Street
Purchase, NY 10577
914.249.2000
www.mastercard.com

Oracle iPayment, *Rules, Decisioning*
500 Oracle Parkway
Redwood Shores, CA 94065
650.506.0794
www.oracle.com

Paymentech, *Fraud Scoring, Identity Authentication, Age Verification*
1601 Elm Street

Dallas, TX 75201
800.708.3740
www.paymentech.com

Quova, *Geolocation*
333 W. Evelyn Avenue
Mountain View, CA 94041
650.528.3700
www.quova.com

Retail Decisions ReD,   *Fraud Scoring, Decisioing*
ReD House
Brookwood
Surrey
GU24 GBL
United Kingdom
+44 1483 728 700
www.redplc.com

RiskWise, *Reverse Lookup, Fraud Scoring*
1010 West Germain Street, Suite 300
St. Cloud, MN 56301
320.203.6600
www.riskwise.com

Sam Spade, *Geolocation (free, limited view)*
www.samspade.org

SearchSpace Corporation, *Fraud Scoring*
60 Broad Street
New York, NY 10004
212.422.5100
www.searchspace.com

TouchCredit, *Biometric*
15 Outrigger Street
Marina Del Rey, CA 90292
310.305.3764
www.touchcredit.com

TransUnion, *Credit Report, Access*
PO Box 2000
Chester, PA 19022
312.466.7363
www.transunion.com

United States Postal Service, *Zip Code Match, Address Verifications*
800.275.8777
www.usps.com

VerifyIDs
866.837.4397
www.verifyids.com

VeriVoice, *Biometric*
5 Vaughn Drive
Princeton, NJ 08540
609.452.9220
www.verivoice.com

Visa, *Authorization, Verified By Visa, Card Security CVV2*
900 Metro Center Blvd
Foster City, CA 94404
800.911.VISA
www.visa.com

XPORTA, *Export Compliance*
275 Saratoga Ave.
Suite 260
Santa Clara, CA 95050
866.490.0853
www.xporta.com

Appendix B

Protecting Identity Theft

The following checklist will help guide you through the steps you can take to protect yourself from being a victim of identity theft.

1. Never leave receipts at bank machines, bank counters, trash receptacles, or unattended gasoline pumps. Keep track of all your paperwork. When you no longer need it, destroy it.
2. Memorize your social security number and all of your passwords. Do not record them on any cards or on anything in your wallet or purse.
3. Call the three credit reporting bureaus listed below and get copies of your credit report at least once a year, or if you are using one of the credit notification services that most credit cards offer, just order a copy of one:
   - You don't have to pay for a credit report if you have been denied credit, are on welfare, have been a victim of identity theft or are unemployed.

> Equifax
> P.O Box 105873
> Atlanta, GA 30348
> Report Fraud (800) 525-6285
> Get Credit Report (800) 685-1111
>
> Experian (formally TRW)
> P.O. Box 2104
> Allen, TX 75013-2104
> Report Fraud (800) 301-7195
> Get Credit Report (888) 397-3742
>
> Transunion Corporation

P.O. Box 34012
Fullerton, CA 92834
Report Fraud (800) 680-7289
Get Credit Report (800) 916-8800

4. Empty your wallet of extra credit cards and IDs. Better yet — cancel the ones you do not use and maintain a list of the ones you do.
5. Never give personal information over the telephone, such as your Social Security number, date of birth, mother's maiden name, credit card number, or bank PIN code unless you initiated the phone call. Protect this data.
6. When you open new accounts, create a real password don't use your mother's maiden name.
7. Promptly remove mail from your mailbox after delivery.
8. Deposit outgoing mail in post office collection mailboxes or at your local post office. Do not leave in unsecured mail receptacles.
9. Shred pre-approved credit applications, credit card receipts, bills and other financial information you don't want before discarding them in the trash or recycling bin.
10. Order a copy of your free personal earnings and benefit statement at the United States Social Security Administration by calling (800) 772-1213 or by using your online estimate tools at www.ssa.gov
11. Notify the Direct Marketing Association that you want to remove your name from the direct mail and phone lists:
    Mail Preference Service
    P.O. Box 9008
    Farmingdale, NY 11735

    Telephone Preference Service
    P.O. Box 9014
    Farmingdale, NY 11735

    Or visit their website at www.the-dma.org
12. Sign all new credit cards upon receipt.
13. Save all credit card receipts and match them against your monthly bills.
14. Be conscious of normal receipt of routine financial statements. Contact the sender if they are not received in the mail.
15. Notify your credit card companies and financial institutions in advance of any change of address or phone number.

16. Never loan your credit cards to anyone else.
17. Never put your credit card or any other financial account number on a postcard or on the outside of an envelope.
18. If you applied for a new credit card and is hasn't arrived in a timely manner, call the bank or credit card company involved.
19. Report all lost or stolen credit cards immediately.
20. Beware of mail or telephone solicitations disguised as promotions offering instant prizes or awards designed solely to obtain your personal information or credit card numbers.
21. Use caution when disclosing information online. For any personal information or for credit card information, make sure the forms are secure — you should see https:// and/or a locked key on the screen.
22. When you subscribe to on-line services you may be asked to confirm your credit card number to open the account or your password do not disclose them to anyone.
23. Only use one credit card for making on-line purchases.
24. Shred returned checks or store in a secure location.
25. Don't preprint your Driver's license number or social security number on your checks.

Appendix C

Sample Strategy

The following strategy is meant for illustrative purpose only, and is not meant to be all-inclusive, nor is it meant to represent any particular vertical market. I have purposely put in as many fraud techniques as I could to give some conceptualization to the use of fraud techniques and business flow.

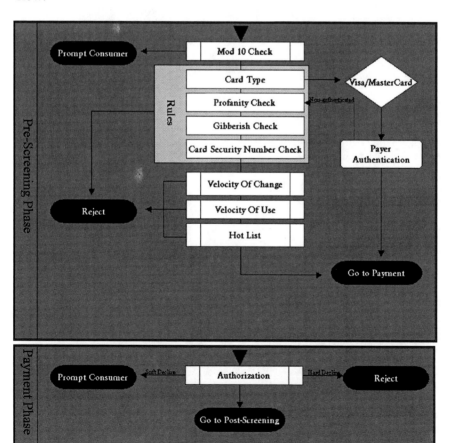

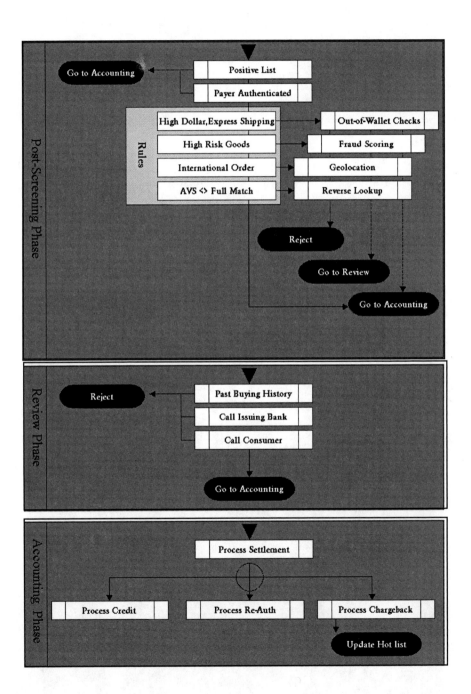

Notes

Index

ISBN 141201460-3

320246